insight text guide

Sue Sherman

Persepolis

Marjane Satrapi

First published in 2018, reprinted in 2019, 2020, 2021, 2023, 2024.

Insight Publications Pty Ltd
3/350 Charman Road
Cheltenham VIC 3192
Australia
Tel: +61 3 8571 4950
Email: books@insightpublications.com.au

www.insightpublications.com.au

A catalogue record for this book is available from the National Library of Australia

ISBNs:
9781925485769 (print)
9781925485776 (digital)

Cover design by Gisela Beer, based on a concept by The Modern Art Production Group

Printed by Markono Print Media Pte Ltd

contents

CHARACTER MAP

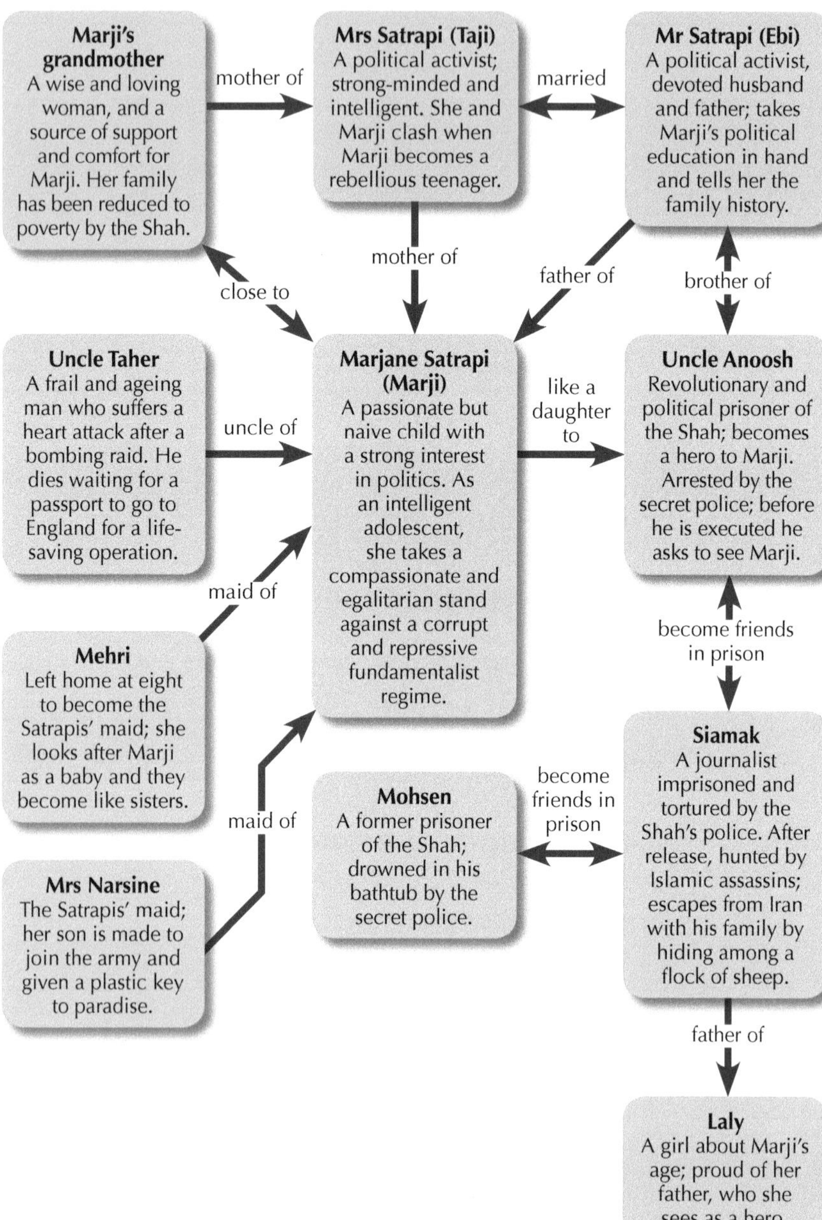

OVERVIEW

About the author

Marjane (Marji) Satrapi was born in Iran in 1969 and grew up in the capital, Tehran. Her family was descended from Persian royalty; her maternal great-grandfather, Nasser-al-Din Shah, was emperor of Persia (1848–1896), and her grandfather was a prince. In twentieth-century Iran, wealthy young Iranians from Marjane's parents' and grandparents' generations studied overseas and some were attracted to Marxist doctrines. Many (including Marjane's parents) became strongly involved in the campaign to overthrow the Shah, Mohammad Reza Pahlavi (Macnab 2006). He was a secular (non-religious) Muslim with policies of Western-style modernisation, but the widespread bribery and corruption of his regime provoked strong public opposition which culminated in the Iranian Revolution of 1979, during which he was deposed and exiled.

The Shah was replaced by the strict religious leader Ayatollah Khomeini, who opposed westernisation and reintroduced sharia law (law based on the Quran). This made life increasingly dangerous for citizens such as Marjane and her family. As a strong-minded young girl, Marjane rebelled against the lack of personal freedom; she objected to discrimination against women and was horrified by the injustice and brutality inflicted on those who opposed the new regime. Some of her relatives and family friends were among those persecuted, arrested and murdered. When her beloved Uncle Anoosh was executed Marjane became more rebellious, publicly ignoring 'modesty' codes and buying banned Western music. In 1983, Marjane's parents, fearing for her safety, sent her to the Lycée Français de Vienne. This part of her life is recounted in the first volume of *Persepolis*.

Persepolis 2 (which is not covered in this text guide) recounts Marjane's high-school years in Vienna, when she lived at times in various friends' homes and also spent two months living on the streets. She returned to Iran after suffering from pneumonia that was so severe she nearly died from it. Back in Iran she studied visual communication, obtaining a master's degree from Islamic Azad University in Tehran.

As a writer and illustrator, Satrapi became internationally famous with her autobiographical graphic novels, originally published in French in four parts in 2000–03. They were translated into English in two parts in 2003 and 2004 as *Persepolis: The Story of a Childhood* and *Persepolis 2: The Story of a Return. Persepolis* has now sold over two million copies and been translated into twelve languages; it won the 2001 Coup de Coeur Award at the Angoulême International Comics Festival, and was ranked by *Newsweek* as number five on its list of the ten best nonfiction books of the decade. Satrapi's book *Embroideries* (*Broderies*) was also nominated for the Angoulême Album of the Year award in 2003, and her novel *Chicken with Plums* (2004) won this award in 2005. The influential website *ComicsAlliance* has listed Satrapi as one of twelve women cartoonists deserving of lifetime achievement recognition.

Persepolis was adapted by Satrapi and director Vincent Paronnaud into a French-language animated film that debuted at the 2007 Cannes Film Festival and shared a Special Jury Prize with *Silent Light*. An English-language version followed, and was nominated for an Academy Award for Best Animated Feature in 2008.

Marjane Satrapi currently lives in Paris and is married to Mattias Ripa, a Swedish actor who stars with her in the film *The Gang of the Jotas* (2013), which she also wrote and directed.

Synopsis

As a child from a wealthy middle-class family during the reign of Shah Reza Pahlavi, Marji Satrapi's life is comfortable but she is aware of the social inequality and political oppression in Iran. An intelligent child with politically active parents, Marji reads Karl Marx's political theories and strongly supports the idea of social justice. She also dreams of becoming a prophet, through which she has childish ambitions of achieving social justice.

Many educated Iranians actively oppose the Shah's tyrannical rule, which causes widespread civil unrest, and numerous people are imprisoned, tortured and executed. During demonstrations against the Shah, government troops massacre hundreds of people. After the Shah is deposed in the revolution of 1979, Marji and her family initially rejoice; Marji's Uncle Anoosh is released from prison and she develops a close relationship with him. However, the new government, headed by the fundamentalist cleric Ayatollah Khomeini, becomes increasingly repressive and ruthless – a threat to everyone who, like the Satrapis, values freedom and independence. Uncle Anoosh is one of many people who are imprisoned. When he is accused of being a Russian spy and executed, Marji is utterly devastated.

Life in Iran becomes more difficult during the war with Iraq. This begins in 1980, with Iraq's random missile strikes and attacks on oil tankers in the Persian Gulf. Iran responds by bombing Iraq and a long and bloody conflict ensues. Many lives are lost in Iran and food becomes scarce in supermarkets. The government brainwashes young peasant boys and lures them into the army with plastic keys painted gold – allegedly to open the gates of paradise when they die in battle. The fundamentalist government also imposes sharia law, which Marji's family often ignores. Thus the family is threatened not only by falling bombs, but also by their devout or fearful neighbours who might report them for un-Islamic behaviour.

Marji's parents holiday in Turkey and bring her back a denim jacket. Wearing the jacket in the street, Marji is confronted by two female Guardians of the Revolution (fundamentalist women) who threaten to report her to the authorities. The war continues and Marji's neighbours are killed when their neighbourhood is bombed. She is very distressed and becomes more openly rebellious, wearing jewellery to school and hitting the Principal when she tries to confiscate Marji's bracelet. She is expelled and, although her parents find her another school, Marji is soon in trouble again for publicly accusing the teacher of lying. Worried that she will be raped and killed (the fate of young unmarried women who are arrested), Marji's parents organise for her to attend a French school in Vienna, Austria. She is only fourteen.

Marji's departure is painful for her and her family. On the night before she leaves, her grandmother spends the night with her. She tells Marji to always be true to herself, and promises to visit her in Vienna but Marji knows that this will not be possible. At the airport there is an emotional farewell between Marji and her parents. From behind the glass departure-area door, Marji turns back for one last glimpse of her parents and sees her distraught mother, who has fainted, being carried away by her father.

Note: to differentiate between the author and the character in the following analysis of the text, the author is referred to as Satrapi, the adult voice who comments on her younger self in the text is referred to as 'Marjane', and the protagonist in the text is called 'Marji'.

Character summaries

Marjane Satrapi

Marji is ten years old when the Islamic fundamentalist government makes wearing the veil compulsory for women and girls. A believer in social justice like her parents, Marji objects strongly to this discrimination. She wants to be actively involved in public protests and reads many books to expand her political knowledge. Her favourite book, *Dialectical Materialism*, introduces her to Marx's socialist theories. Marji becomes more outspoken and rebellious and is attracted to Western cultural icons such as Kim Wilde and Iron Maiden. At school she openly challenges government propaganda and mocks religious rituals. Worried that she is in danger of being arrested, her parents send her to school in Vienna.

Mrs Satrapi (Taji)

Marji's mother is a strong and outspoken woman. She protests publicly against both the Shah's and the Islamic fundamentalists' oppressive regimes. She is also a strong disciplinarian, punishing Marji severely for disobedience. When Taji is abused and threatened in the street for not wearing a veil, she is deeply upset and becomes ill. While encouraging Marji's independence, Taji also wants to protect her headstrong daughter.

Mr Satrapi (Ebi)

Marji's father takes part in many political protests with his wife. He also takes photographs of riots, which is illegal and extremely dangerous. Ebi is very knowledgeable about Iran's history and politics. He tells Marji the truth when she repeats propaganda she hears at school and on television. Despite his socialist sympathies, he opposes his young maid's relationship with a neighbour's son because of their class differences. He is a loving husband and father, a passionate patriot and a loyal friend.

Uncle Anoosh

Ebi's brother Anoosh is released from prison after the fall of the Shah. He and Marji form a strong bond of affection and he tells her his story. At eighteen, Anoosh joined his uncle Fereydoon, who had proclaimed independence from the Shah by forming a separatist republic in Azerbaijan. The Shah's soldiers attacked and Anoosh fled to the USSR, where he married and had two children. He was homesick, however, and returned to Iran, where he was quickly arrested and imprisoned for nine years. After his release, Anoosh is arrested by Islamic authorities, and executed as a Russian spy.

Marji's grandmother

A kind and loving woman who has a close relationship with her granddaughter, Marji's grandmother tells Marji stories of her past, and about living in poverty after the Shah's father took all their possessions.

The night before Marji leaves for Vienna, her grandmother comes to stay and they share a bed. Marji is comforted by the warmth of her grandmother's presence and is distraught at leaving her.

Siamak Jari and Mohsen Shakiba

Siamak and Mohsen are both political prisoners of the Shah's regime. They become friends in prison. When they are released, Siamak is reunited with his wife and daughter. Mohsen is killed – drowned in his bathtub – by fundamentalist assassins who then search for Siamak, and kill his sister when they cannot find him. Siamak and his family flee across the border, hidden among a flock of sheep.

BACKGROUND & CONTEXT

Historical and political setting

Persepolis refers to the ancient capital of Persia (Iran). From 550 to 330 BC, the Persian Empire of Cyrus the Great spanned three continents. By 480 BC it was the largest empire the world had ever seen, with a seat of power in Peris (Persepolis), and ruling over an estimated 112.4 million people. In 330 BC, Alexander the Great conquered the city of Persepolis; he seized its treasures and burned the city to the ground.

The Muslim conquest of Persia (633–56 AD) was a key period in Iranian history. The Islamisation of Iran occurred during the eighth to tenth centuries and was a significant factor in the ultimate decline of its traditional religion, Zarathustrianism (also called Zoroastrianism). Much later, the nearby Russian Empire took over many of Iran's territories during and following the Russo–Persian Wars of 1804–13 and 1826–28.

In 1941 (during World War II) the German army successfully attacked Russia and the Iranian government thought that Germany would win the war. Fighting against Germany were the Allies, including Russia and Britain, who demanded that Iran expel German residents. Iran had declared itself to be neutral and the Shah refused the Allies' demand. This led to an invasion of Iran by Russia and Britain, who easily overwhelmed the Iranian army and gained access to Iranian oil fields, guaranteeing Allied supply lines for the remainder of the war.

When the war ended, Soviet troops stationed in north-western Iran not only refused to withdraw but supported the newly established pro-Soviet separatist states in Iran's northern regions. These were eventually overthrown and Iranian nationalists demanded an end to British control of the oil industry, which was placed under Iranian government ownership and control. The Shah was stripped of his power and reduced to a figurehead. The United States' Central Intelligence Agency (CIA), an organisation that gathers information from around the world for America's national security, organised a coup and restored the Shah to power. This gave the US a political presence in the Middle East, where many Arab nations were inclined to support Russia.

In the 'White Revolution' Muhammad Reza Shah Pahlavi (the Shah of Iran from 1941 to 1979) promoted education, improved social welfare services and gave women the right to vote. At the same time, however, he enforced rigid control over the government through a brutal secret police force. The Shah also applied martial law (military control over the people); he imposed book censorship; mosque libraries were raided; and the army was ordered to open fire on protesters at public demonstrations (see pages 39–40 in the text).

In January and February 1979, after mass demonstrations, strikes and riots, the Shah was overthrown and forced into exile (pp.41–2). The fundamentalist Islamic cleric Ayatollah Khomeini, who himself had been in exile for fifteen years, returned and declared Iran an Islamic Republic. He became the country's leader and the veil became compulsory headwear for females in schools and in all public spaces (referred to, for example, on pages 3 and 98).

The author's historical and political context

The author's historical context encompasses both ancient and modern Iran. Satrapi values her nation's proud heritage and condemns the tyranny imposed on her people through successive invasions over the centuries: those by Iran's own emperors, by Arabs from the west, by Mongolians from the east and finally by modern imperialists. As the child of 'avant-garde' parents (p.6) who are politically active, Satrapi's religious beliefs sometimes come into conflict with her parents' opposition to the Shah and their rejection of the veil. As the repressive Islamic regime takes a stronger hold, Satrapi becomes rebellious and more involved in political activism. As a teenager, she is drawn to the freedom and excitement of American culture.

The following list provides a brief summary of some of the significant political events described in *Persepolis*.

Cinema Rex fire, 19 August 1978 (pp.14–15)

An estimated 470 lives were lost when the Cinema Rex in Abadan (Iran) was set alight. The government blamed the Islamic militants, while the anti-Shah protesters blamed the governmental intelligence service. *Persepolis* endorses the view that Islamic militants were responsible.

Black Friday, 8 September 1979 (pp.38–9)

The massacre of peaceful protestors in Zhaleh Square in Tehran by Iranian government soldiers extinguished any hope of reconciliation between the Shah's regime and the revolutionary movement.

Closing of universities, 1979 (p.73)

After the 1979 revolution the country's sixteen universities were closed. They reopened after the Cultural Revolution but a strict Islamic curriculum was introduced and closely supervised.

Iraq bombs Tehran, 1985 (p.80, pp.103–4)

In 1985, Iraqi warplanes bombed Tehran and two other Iranian cities in largely residential areas. Iraq said the raids were 'retaliation' for an attempt to assassinate the Emir of Kuwait.

Western sexual revolution, 1960s–1980s

Many Western counties were becoming more tolerant and sexually permissive. The contraceptive pill allowed women more sexual freedom; abortion was legalised; and there was a greater acceptance of homosexuality and other sexual identities. (Marji's attraction to Western culture is shown in the chapter 'Kim Wilde', pp.126–34).

Islam

Islam is a religion that believes in one god (Allah), and its teachings and beliefs are contained in the Quran (also written in roman letters as Koran or Qur'an), which is the word of Allah spoken to the prophet Muhammad by the angel Gabriel. The Islamic faith is a nonviolent one, with the Quran emphasising 'the paths of peace' (Quran, 5:16). Gender equality is enshrined in Islamic teaching – 'each of you is equal to the other' (Quran, 3:195), and several Islamic countries have had female heads of state, including Pakistan, Indonesia, Bangladesh and Turkey.

Marxism

The term Marxism refers to the political, economic and social theories of Karl Marx, an influential nineteenth-century philosopher. He argued that, throughout history, change has always been brought about by class struggle between the bourgeoisie (the wealthy; the owners of business and capital) and the proletariat (the workers) – in other words, between the oppressors and the oppressed. Marx predicted that eventually a proletarian revolution would establish a socialist society in which the state would own the means of production, and goods and services would be distributed equally. In the ideal Marxist world, the state would wither away and a communist utopia would emerge.

GENRE, STRUCTURE & LANGUAGE

Genre

Persepolis can be categorised as a **memoir** or an **autobiography** because it is the author's account of real events in her life. As it covers her transition from childhood to adolescence, it is also a **rite of passage** account. It is written in the form of a graphic novel or, as Satrapi prefers to call it, a **comic**.

Memoir and narrative voice

A memoir or autobiography conventionally uses the **first-person narrative voice** and readers see all events from the narrator's perspective. In fact, the narrative of *Persepolis* is more complex than this suggests, and there are three narrative 'voices' in the text:

- Marji, the child
- Marjane, the adult
- Satrapi, the artist.

The **primary narrative voice** is that of Marji, the character in the illustrations. Her narrative voice often engages the reader's sympathy for her vulnerability. For example, when Anoosh fails to collect Marji from school, her anxiety about his safety is conveyed through her tentative questions and abrupt comments (p.67).

The **adult voice** of Marjane in text boxes above the illustrations often reflects on her younger self. For example, on page 10 Marjane comments that, 'The year of the revolution I had to take action. So I put my prophetic destiny aside for a while.' She is able to see beyond Marji's limited view of the world. Her wider perspective brings a historical and political backdrop to Marji's story and gives readers a sense of the hard road ahead for the eager child who wants to change the world.

Satrapi's **authorial voice** is also evident in her artwork, which clearly conveys her views. On page 6, for example, a dividing line through Marji's body separates her conflicting worlds. Marji is torn between her 'very religious' self, and the 'avant-garde' world of her parents. In the left half of the frame are symbols of progressive society where Marji can become what she later describes as 'an educated, liberated woman' (p.73). The right half of the frame evokes a traditional Muslim world, where Marji's gender will limit her options; yet this world is alluring, as shown by the graceful curves and flourishes of Islamic art. Satrapi's illustrations add a deeper level of meaning, emphasising the way Marji is caught between two worlds.

In a memoir, narrators confide in readers by sharing their private thoughts and feelings. In the following quotation we see Marji's sorrow at leaving her country, her home and her parents; and we sympathise strongly with her deep sense of loss.

> I repeated what [my parents] had told me over and over in my head. I was pretty sure they weren't coming to Vienna. I stayed up all night and wondered if the moon shone as brightly in Vienna. (p.149)

Graphic novel / comic

Persepolis is also a graphic novel or a comic (the latter being Satrapi's preferred term for describing the text), and its meaning is conveyed by the illustrations as much as by the words. On page 15, for example, the many ghost-like figures almost completely filling the frame convey the horror of their deaths, trapped inside the locked theatre which has been set alight. Their ascending bodies resemble the flames that consume them, as other doomed people rush frantically towards the locked exits. The stark visual imagery emphasises the cruelty of their killers, while the written text provides a more concrete description of the events.

The genre of the comic dates back to storytelling on fabric, when panels of tapestry would relate and celebrate the battles and successes of royalty. While her work utilises generic features of the comic, Satrapi does not follow the conventions of medieval tapestries that celebrate the heroic actions of a protagonist. Instead, she portrays herself in *Persepolis* as someone who gives a voice to those who have been silenced or marginalised.

Structure

The structure of *Persepolis* is mostly **linear**, with events recounted in chronological order, beginning when Marji is ten (but remembering events from when she was six) and ending when she is fourteen. There are nineteen chapters, each one dealing with a particular political event and/or personal crisis.

The political events are cataclysmic – beginning with the revolutionary events leading to the Shah's downfall. Acts of violence, injustice and corruption drive the narrative, and individual deeds of rebellion (especially by Marji and her family) create narrative tension. There is no single dramatic climax, but the narrative includes a series of alarming crises. An example is Marji's father's late arrival home after illegally photographing a demonstration. These crises often end in tragedy (such as the deaths of Taher and Anoosh). There is no traditionally satisfactory resolution at the conclusion of the narrative, rather a sense that the story is unfinished.

Verbal language

The language used by the various characters reveals aspects of their personalities. Marji's public contradiction of her teacher, for example, shows her fearlessness (and perhaps recklessness) in revealing the truth:

> You say that we don't have political prisoners anymore. But we've gone from 800 prisoners under the Shah to 300,000 under your regime. How dare you lie to us like that? (p.144)

Conversations reveal relationships between characters. Siamak and Mohsen recall their torture in prison, which included beatings with electric cables, cigarettes being extinguished on their backs and thighs, and the burning of a prisoner with an iron (p.51). There is a sense of camaraderie in their recounting of these horrific details. The conversation reveals their enormous courage and their loyalty to and affection for each other.

The language used in Marji's private thoughts is also revealing: for example, she reflects on the tragic fate of Niloufar, a 'real martyr', whose blood 'certainly did not feed our society's veins' (p.146). Marji's language reveals her compassion for Niloufar and her bitter cynicism about the government's political rhetoric.

Another aspect of the verbal language of the text is Satrapi's explicit condemnation of political duplicity, in both the Shah's regime and the Islamic Republic. For example, schoolchildren are told that the King (Shah) was chosen by God (p.19), but after he is deposed they are ordered to tear his photo from their books (p.44).

Political rhetoric is another example of dishonest and controlling language. To justify the terrible slaughter of young men in the unequal battle against Iraq, the people are told that 'to die a martyr is to inject blood into the veins of society' (p.146). The reality is that 'the survival of the regime' depended on the needless sacrifice of the lives of 'a million people' (p.116).

Visual language

The visual features of the text, such as the black-and-white figures and the apparent simplicity with which they are drawn, help readers to relate to the complex political setting and the text's philosophical ideas. The images are often stark, as befitting the harsh subject matter, and the sharpness of the black-and-white contrasts tends to dramatise the actions and expressions of the characters.

The illustrations in *Persepolis* have been likened to German Expressionist art from the beginning of the twentieth century. One way in which these two visual art forms are connected is through the similarity of the themes they explore; the following list identifies three examples of classic Expressionist themes and ideas in *Persepolis*.

- Class difference and oppression are shown in the illustration of socially disadvantaged youth 'exploding' on the battlefield (p.102).
- The merging of fantasy with reality is shown in the 'magic carpet' escape to Italy and Spain (p.77).
- A 'nightmarish' aspect is evident in more violent panels, such as the fire at the Cinema Rex (p.15).

These features contribute to a sense of profound alienation and personal displacement, characteristic of German Expressionism. This is most strikingly captured in the illustration of Marji floating in space after the execution of Anoosh (p.71). The influence of monochrome woodcut prints is evocative of the Die Brücke Expressionist artists who, as characterised by art historian Peter Selz, are 'driven by an inner need' to express personal feelings and to 'project unresolved conflicts in society' (cited in Copley 2011).

Satrapi's **juxtapositions of scale** are also suggestive of the menacing atmosphere in Expressionist art: two examples are the rescuers being dwarfed by the giant policemen who guard the locked doors to the burning cinema (p.14), and the Guardians of the Revolution looming ominously over Marji in the street (pp.132–3). In her use of black and white, Satrapi rejects the vivid colours of traditional comic illustrations. The black-and-white clothing of the characters avoids particular emphasis on any one person, allowing readers to more easily identify with all characters, regardless of their age or gender, and allows Satrapi to 'speak' on behalf of the community. As Jessica Copley suggests, in merging stylistic features of Expressionism with those of comic art, Satrapi 'maintains an ethical distance by avoiding realistic representation' that might 'degrade and intrude upon the memory of victims' (Copley 2011).

Symbols

Many of the objects and images in *Persepolis* are symbolic; the following list explains some of the more important symbols.

- **Blood** signifies suffering and loss. For example, the blood of 'martyrs' (p.115) implies the government's celebration of their heroism but Satrapi sees it as slaughter. The many 'red crescent trucks' outside the hospital (p.120) show the government's insatiable need for its citizens' blood, and make it seem monstrous.
- **Books** symbolise the pursuit of knowledge and the gaining of wisdom (pp.32–3).
- **Cigarettes** are symbolic of entry into the world of adults (p.117).
- **Clothing** reflects an individual's identity and allegiance to a wider group. Western clothing symbolises Marji's defiance of the Islamic regime – veils and body-covering clothing represent submission. Ebi's tie (p.108) and Marji's denim jacket (p.133) symbolise – to the Guardians of the Revolution – Western decadence.
- **Hair** also reflects identity and an individual's values; it can be regarded in different ways depending on the viewer's ideology. For example, women's uncovered hair symbolises (to fundamentalists) their sexual allure. For non-fundamentalists, on the other hand, it symbolises personal freedom and gender equality.
- **Jewellery** can symbolise social status or resistance to authority. The jewellery Marji wears to school symbolises her defiance of fundamentalist oppression (p.143). Neda's turquoise bracelet, Mali's jewellery (p.90) and the jewellery sold in shops (p.138) symbolise the social divide in Iran.
- **Keys to Paradise** are plastic, gold-painted keys given to sons of the poor. They also symbolise the social divide and reveal the government's dishonesty and inhumanity (pp.99–102).
- **Music**, usually played at parties and often accompanied by dancing, symbolises enjoyment and celebration (p.106).

- **Parties** are illegal in fundamentalist Iran; usually involving alcohol, they are symbolic of resistance to fundamentalism.
- **Swans made of bread** symbolise beauty, and the strength of the human spirit. Despite tragic circumstances, Anoosh creates works of art from scraps of bread. The swans also symbolise the transformative power of art amidst suffering and deprivation.
- **Wine** is symbolic of freedom and enjoyment, and usually connected with parties. It also symbolises resistance to fundamentalist oppression.

Irony

Irony occurs when there is a tension or contradiction between what is literally stated and what the actual meaning is. Examples of irony in *Persepolis* include the following.

- Marji's initial enjoyment of Monopoly – a game that endorses the capitalist pursuit of money – is particularly ironic, as Karl Marx is one of her heroes and his ideals oppose capitalism.
- Mohsen's joke about his ability to survive (p.50) is ironic as he is subsequently drowned in his bathtub by Islamic fundamentalists (p.65).
- Ebi's need for a drink (a 'pick-me-up', p.110) to calm his nerves after all his wine has been flushed away so that he won't be arrested is ironic (pp.108–10). Further irony is evident in the fact that Ebi's bribery of the police makes the loss of the wine unnecessary.

Some of Satrapi's irony is **humorous**, inviting readers to smile at Marji's naivety or exaggeration; and some – such as Mohsen's 'joke' (p.50) – is **tragic**. Satrapi's political censure is sometimes conveyed through irony: for example, the illustration of the young boys exploding on the battlefields, juxtaposed with one of teenagers dancing at a party, is a condemnation of social injustice (p.102).

CHAPTER-BY-CHAPTER ANALYSIS

The veil (pp.3–9)

Summary: *The text begins with images of ten-year-old Marji and her classmates wearing veils. They don't like the veil and don't understand why they have to wear it. Marji wishes to become a prophet so she can eradicate social inequality; in bed at night, she has discussions with God.*

The chapter's first frame shows Marji alone and, in the second, she has been cut from the group photo (p.3). This indicates her separateness from her classmates – both as a politically aware child, and as an individual who will stand against political oppression. Marji's parents are politically active and, although she is proud of her mother's public opposition to the veil, Marji is also 'very religious' and is not sure 'what to think' (p.6). Her challenging journey will involve her developing her own moral frameworks within which she can situate her beliefs and ideals.

Key point

Her grandmother's belief in her gives Marji the confidence to hold onto her dream of becoming a prophet. Marji's need for self-belief becomes increasingly necessary as her familiar world falls apart.

Key vocabulary

Capitalism: the economic system in countries like the US and Australia, in which profit and private ownership drive trade and industry.

Avant-garde: modern, experimental, unconventional.

Cadillac: an expensive American car.

Zarathustra: an ancient prophet, also known as Zoroaster; Zarathustrianism (or Zoroastrianism) is a monotheistic religion (believing in one god).

Q In what ways is Iran's new fundamentalist regime portrayed as being worse than the old one ruled by the Shah?

The bicycle (pp.10–17)

Summary: *Dressed as Che Guevara, Marji plays revolutionary games with her friends. She reads a comic book called* Dialectical Materialism *(p.12), which summarises the theories of philosophers such as René Descartes and social reformers including Karl Marx. Marji overhears her parents talking about the fire at the Cinema Rex. A public protest is planned and Marji begs her mother to take her. Taji refuses and Marji calls on God for help but he doesn't appear.*

Marji's confession that her faith is 'not unshakeable' (rather, it can sometimes be questioned) suggests that her horizons have been broadened by her acquisition of knowledge. Tragic events during the Vietnam War and, closer to home, the burning of the Cinema Rex have shown her the vulnerability of innocent civilians living in a war zone, and the manipulation of the truth for political purposes. Marji is inspired by revolutionaries such as Castro with his egalitarian communist ideology. Illustrations from her comic-book version of *Dialectical Materialism* show Marx and Descartes discussing whether a stone exists or is simply imagined (p.13). Descartes' experience of pain when Marx throws the rock at him is evidence that the rock exists. Marji's question to God – 'where are you?' (p.17) – suggests her need for Him to prove His existence to her as Marx has demonstrated the existence of the rock.

Key point

Marji's simplistic analogy of the bicycle ignores the violence of revolution. Her difficult political awakening comes with her exposure to the human suffering caused by violent conflict.

Key vocabulary

Che Guevara: an Argentine Marxist revolutionary doctor, guerrilla leader and diplomat. His image has come to symbolise the revolutionary spirit.

Descartes: René Descartes, a seventeenth-century French philosopher who questioned everything in order to find something that was absolutely certain. He eventually decided that 'I exist' is impossible to doubt.

Dialectical Materialism: a critique of capitalism by French philosopher and activist Henri Lefebvre (1901–1991). Marji reads a comic book of the same name.

Fidel Castro: the political revolutionary then leader of Cuba (1959–2008) who defied America and turned his country into a communist state.

Karl Marx: see 'Marxism' on page 10 of this guide.

The children of Palestine: a reference to the suffering of Palestinian children caught up in the Israeli–Palestinian conflict.

The Iranian revolutionaries: Fatemeh Rezaï, Dr Hossein Fatemi and Hamid Ashraf were executed for their political beliefs and actions.

'Young Vietnamese killed by Americans': a reference to the Vietnam War (1955–75). For instance, in the Mỹ Lai Massacre in 1968, between 347 and 504 unarmed South Vietnamese civilians, including children, were killed by US soldiers.

Q Select one of the frames in this chapter and explain how its visual language adds information or expresses an emotion that is not conveyed by the frame's verbal language.

The water cell (pp.18–25)

Summary: *Marji is upset when her parents demonstrate against the King (Shah) because her teacher has told her that the King was 'chosen by God' (p.19). Her father tells her the 'truth' (p.19). A soldier named Reza organised a 'putsch' (a military uprising) to overthrow the Emperor (p.19). He became the first Shah. Marji's grandfather had been a prince but the Shah made him prime minister. When her grandfather became a communist, the Shah imprisoned and tortured him – confining him for many hours in a cell full of water. Wanting to experience his suffering, Marji takes a long bath.*

Marji learns the difference between the propaganda she is told at school and the truth her parents tell her, but still wants to believe that God helped the Shah. When Marji's grandfather becomes the Shah's prime minister he meets foreign intellectuals and becomes aware of social injustice, which leads him to embrace communism. For this he is frequently imprisoned. Through Marji's narrative perspective, we are positioned to admire her family's history of egalitarian values as well as their courage. Marji's mimicking of the heroic suffering of her grandfather's water-cell torture is a test of her own capacity for courage to oppose evil.

Key point

Marji's journey towards political maturity is reflected in her sudden lack of interest in the Monopoly game at the end of the chapter. Indeed, her initial enjoyment of a game that endorses the capitalist pursuit of money and property is highly ironic, especially for a child who idolises Karl Marx.

Q Why is Marji so delighted by her connection to royalty?

Persepolis (pp.26–32)

Summary: *Marji learns about the poverty her grandmother suffered when the original Shah took all their possessions. With only bread to eat, her grandmother pretended to cook so the neighbours would think they had proper food. Marji's father returns home late from illegally photographing a demonstration and talks about the young man killed by the police. As his body is carried from the hospital, the assembled crowd proclaims him a martyr. When the body of an old man is carried out, and he is also proclaimed a martyr, the man's wife objects, saying that her husband died of cancer.*

Marji's thanks to God for her father's safe return show her need for something to believe in when danger threatens. At the hospital, the crowd's celebration of the man who died of cancer suggests their need for heroes. The widow's sudden agreement with the crowd causes Marji's family great amusement, much to Marji's bewilderment. She suddenly realises that she doesn't 'understand anything' (p.32). Marji's laughter at her own ignorance leads her to read all the books she can find.

Key point

The amusement of Marji's family shows their awareness that the distortion of truth can sometimes be absurd. Yet there is a kind of wry (twisted) humour in the notion that the Shah can be blamed for anything harmful – even when it's known to be untrue.

The letter (pp.33–9)

Summary: *The Satrapis' maid, Mehri, falls in love with the neighbour's son, Hossein, whom she sees through his window, and they exchange letters. Marji's father finds out; he tells Hossein that Mehri is not his daughter but only the maid; Hossein quickly loses interest. Marji comforts Mehri by slipping into bed with her at night. Marji takes Mehri to a dangerous demonstration (later known as 'Black Friday') and her angry mother slaps their faces.*

Marji's social conscience expands and, although she can do nothing to help poor children who are forced to work to help their families, she tries to help Mehri by writing letters to Hossein for her. This shows her naive idealism in imagining that the son of a wealthy neighbour would be interested in a servant. She is shocked when her father, a firm believer in social justice, adheres to socially constructed class boundaries that discriminate against the poor.

Key point

With no access to education, Mehri takes social inequality for granted. By contrast, educated children like Marji can recognise and challenge discrimination, as she does with her objection to the veil (p.3), and her ambition to become a prophet (p.6).

Key vocabulary

Ali Ashraf Darvishian: an Iranian writer who lived from 1941 to 2017. As a schoolteacher he worked in poor villages, and he took up social and cultural concerns in his writing.

Charles Dickens: a nineteenth-century English writer and social critic. He is best known for novels such as *Great Expectations,* which often showed poor characters as virtuous and honest.

Republic: a system of government in which power is not held by a king or emperor, but by the people and their elected representatives.

Q Why do you think the values demonstrated by Ebi's attitude to Mehri might differ from the more idealistic principles he usually expresses?

The party (pp.40–6)

Summary: *The Shah is forced into exile, and celebrations erupt throughout the country. The schools, which had closed during the revolution, now reopen. Marji wants to punish one of her schoolfriends whose father was a member of the Shah's secret police. Marji's mother explains that she must learn forgiveness.*

Marji's neighbours boast of a bullet wound which the wife allegedly received at a demonstration against the Shah but Marji's family knows it is a lie. It seems that people in the new Iran want to prove their opposition to the Shah. Marji and her friends try to punish Ramin, son of a member of the Savak (the Shah's secret police), but Ramin justifies his father's actions because he believed the communists he killed were 'evil' (p.46). Marji's mother explains that he believes what he is told (as Marji sometimes does).

Key point

Marji's need to punish Ramin is an echo of the cycle of political reprisals in Iran, firstly by the Shah and then by the Islamic fundamentalists. The children's mimicry of adults' acts of revenge is a disturbing sign of how deeply ingrained the need for revenge can become.

Key vocabulary

The Middle East: a region that includes Arab countries such as Bahrain, Cyprus, Egypt, Iran, Iraq, Jordan and Kuwait.

Q To what extent does an individual's belief that he or she is right justify an evil act?

Q How do you interpret the image of the serpent-like creature in the frame on page 43?

The heroes (pp.47–53)

Summary: *Laly and her mother visit the Satrapis. Laly's father, Siamak, is absent and Marji tells her he is dead. When Siamak is freed from jail, he and his family visit the Satrapis. Another ex-prisoner, Mohsen, visits and the men talk about torture and death. Marji invents a torture games to play with her friends, but is 'overwhelmed' by the diabolical feeling of power she experiences when she looks in the mirror (p.53). Her mother tells her that the bad people will pay (p.53), which confuses Marji, who now knows about forgiveness; she abandons* Dialectic Materialism *and seeks comfort in God.*

Marji's need for the 'truth' takes precedence over Laly's need for hope that her father is still alive. Marji learns that there is a time for speaking the truth and a time for remaining silent. She listens to the men describing horrific torture and devises torture games to help her understand the effects of torture. Although her childish imaginings are absurdly inadequate in evoking real torture, she gains some sense of its horror. Marji's reconnection with God shows her need for comfort in a disturbing world.

Key point

Marji encounters some of the complex moral questions that arise in times of conflict. She learns that the need for justice can override the need for forgiveness. As her mother explains, 'bad people are dangerous', but so is 'forgiving them' (p.53).

Q Does Marji's 'diabolical' enjoyment of power suggest that power is essentially evil?

Moscow (pp.54–61)

Summary: *Marji is disappointed that her father is not a hero. When she meets her heroic uncle, Anoosh, she loves him 'immediately' (p.54). He tells her of joining his uncle Fereydoon in the resistance movement in Azerbaijan; when the Shah's soldiers crushed Fereydoon's rebellion Anoosh escaped to Russia and later returned to Iran in disguise. He was recognised and imprisoned for nine years. He gives Marji a swan, which he made from bread while in prison.*

Marji's admiration of heroes predisposes her to love her uncle, Anoosh. Her satisfaction that his imprisonment was longer than Laly's father's gives her – she thinks – a moral victory over Laly. As a child growing up in a brutal war zone, young Marji's world is populated by heroes and villains, and aligning herself with heroes makes her feel strong. Marji also needs to reclaim her self-esteem, which was diminished by Laly's implicit criticism of her family.

Key point

The stories Marji hears become central to her own story, and are part of a violent period in Iran's turbulent history. As the author of *Persepolis*, Marji follows the storytelling traditions of her family.

Q Is Satrapi critical of her younger self for her competitiveness with Laly? What does this chapter reveal about her and the world she lives in?

The sheep (pp.62–71)

Summary: *Many members of Marji's family leave Iran. Mohsen is murdered by having his head held underwater. Anoosh still tries to believe that 'everything will be alright' (p.65). Siamak and his family escape, hiding among a flock of sheep. Anoosh is arrested and is allowed one visitor; he asks to see Marji and gives her another bread swan. He is executed as a Russian spy. When God appears in Marji's room she shouts at him to get out.*

When she sees the newspaper report about Anoosh's death Marji bitterly recalls his words of hope; she angrily rejects God, who is no longer able to comfort and reassure her. When the war with Iraq erupts, Marji's sense of desolation at the utter disintegration of her world is vividly conveyed by the illustration on page 74, with the small figure of Marji adrift in a cosmic darkness.

Key point

The newspaper headline labelling Anoosh a 'Russian spy' (p.70) exemplifies the way in which language can be used for political gain. As well as punishing a dissenter, the government's propaganda suggests that it is protecting Iran against the 'evil' of communism.

The trip (pp.72–9)

Summary: *Islamic fundamentalists occupy the US embassy; schools and universities are closed because of their 'decadent' ideas (p.73). In the street, Taji is confronted by fundamentalists and threatened with rape for not wearing a veil. Marji and her family attend a demonstration against fundamentalism and the protesters are savagely attacked. Marji and her family take a trip to Italy while they can still travel freely. On their return home, Marji's grandmother informs them that Iraq has invaded Iran.*

Marji is disturbed that the increasingly restrictive fundamentalist regime in Iran will prevent her from studying chemistry at university. Taji becomes ill after the attack in the street, and many terrified women wear the chador in public (fully covering their bodies, apart from their faces), implicitly condoning the notion of women's intrinsic seductiveness. At a public demonstration against the veil, Marji sees, for the first time, the shocking violence of the fundamentalists as they silence opponents.

Key point

Marji's desire to fight for her country shows her passion for political causes. She is outraged that Arabs 'kept attacking' (p.79), yet it's only the second Arab invasion in 1400 years. Satrapi portrays young Marji's tendency to overreact in an amusing light.

Q Why is Taji uninterested in the occupation of the American embassy (p.72)?

The F-14s (pp.80–6)

Summary: *Iraqi F-14 fighter jets bomb Tehran. On the television, the Iranian news service announces Iran's retaliatory bombing of Iraq but the BBC radio broadcast reveals that there were heavy Iranian losses. Marji worries for her friend, Pardisse, whose father is a pilot who is killed in the raid. At school, Pardisse gives a moving talk about her father; later she tells Marji she would prefer him to be alive and in jail instead of being a dead hero.*

Taji's obliviousness to the bombing prompts an authorial comment from Satrapi that 'war always takes you by surprise' (p.81). This ironic understatement suggests the unpredictability of life in the midst of war – a point tragically made when the Baba-Levys are killed (p.142). That evening, Marji and her parents are 'overwhelmed' – both Marji and her father are moved to tears – by the playing of Iran's national anthem on television (p.83). Marji and Ebi are overjoyed at the bombing of Baghdad; their disregard for Iraqi civilian lives is ironic, given their own experience of being bombed. This reveals the extent to which ongoing hostilities between the two nations have instilled bitterness and hatred between them.

Key point

Marji's father explains that the 'real Islamic invasion' of Iran is not by Iraq but by Iran's own government (p.81). He is referring to the way that one oppressive regime has been replaced by another, promising a better society but delivering a much worse one.

Key vocabulary

BBC: the British Broadcasting Corporation, which provides a worldwide news service with a reputation for reliability and integrity.

Q How does this chapter use humour to heighten the impact of tragic events?

The jewels (pp.87–93)

Summary: *Supermarket shelves in Tehran are mostly empty and women fight over what is available. The oil refinery at Abadan is bombed and the Satrapis fear for the safety of a family friend, Mali, who lives in Abadan with her family. Mali and her family arrive, having lost everything but a few jewels, which they sell to buy food. At the supermarket, some local women complain about refugees causing greater food shortages; they also accuse the 'southern' women of selling their bodies.*

At the supermarket, a joke about kidney beans and 'flatulence' makes life seem less miserable. Mali's two young sons cannot stop saying 'fart' and dissolving into helpless laughter. Mali, however, is deeply upset by the spiteful slur on 'southern' women. She says that although losing everything in a bombing raid is dreadful, being 'spat upon by your own kind' is 'intolerable' (p.93).

Key point

The women in the supermarket who fight over food items and insult Mali show how quickly people can turn on each other. Marji is 'ashamed' (p.93) of the way refugees are treated in Tehran.

Q What do Marji's interactions with the younger boys in this chapter tell you about her character?

The key (pp.94–102)

Summary: *Iran's supply of soldiers compensates for Iraq's superior weaponry, as Marji sombrely notes, looking at the long list of 'war martyrs' in the newspaper (p.94). At school, the students are encouraged to beat themselves to show religious fervour; men sometimes use chains or even knives. At home, Mrs Nasrine, the maid, shows Marji and Taji a gold-painted plastic key, allegedly to paradise, for martyrs who die in battle. Marji goes to her first teenage party.*

When Marji mocks the flagellation rituals at school she is reprimanded by the teacher. Other students join in the 'rebellion' and parents are called in, but they complain about the school's indoctrination and repression of their children. The sons of the poor, by contrast, are called upon to die for their country. Naive fourteen-year-old boys are promised 'plenty of ... women' in paradise if they become martyrs (p.100). The fact that only the sons of the poor are given these keys stirs Marji's Marxist sentiments.

Key point

The juxtaposition of the two frames on the final page of the chapter makes a powerful point. Poor boys with plastic keys around their necks die in battle, while the sons and daughters of the affluent dance at a party. The similarity of the central male figures' actions in each frame reinforces this point.

Key vocabulary

Flagellation: the act of whipping, especially for religious purposes.

The wine (pp.103–10)

Summary: *Taji puts up black curtains after a friend's home is raided by the Guardians of the Revolution and the husband is given seventy-five lashes for possessing 'banned' items (p.105). Driving home from a party, Marji's family is stopped by armed Guardians, who accuse her father of having been drinking. The Guardians accompany them home to check for illegal alcohol. Marji and her grandmother rush ahead and pour all the alcohol down the toilet, but her father bribes the men and they go away.*

The bombing of Tehran brings the residents of Marji's apartment building together and a strong sense of community is evident as they huddle in the basement. The danger is not just from Iraqi bombs, however; it is also from neighbourhood spies and the fanatical Guardians of the Revolution. It is a sign of ordinary people's resistance to oppression that many of them continue to drink alcohol. There is even humour to be found in potential disaster – such as the fact that the alcohol that has just been poured down the toilet is exactly what Ebi needs to help him recover from his ordeal.

Key point

The banning of items such as records and videos, and the excessively harsh penalties for possessing them, suggests that religious fundamentalism is more about power than piety. The fact that the Guardians of the Revolution can be bribed also casts great doubt on their religious commitment.

Q To what extent do you think Marji hides her own fear?

The cigarette (pp.111–17)

Summary: *At school, twelve-year-old Marji mixes with older girls. They skip class and go to a popular cafe – where they check out the boys. Arriving home, Marji is in trouble with her mother for missing class. She accuses her mother of being a dictator and spends time in the basement; she thinks about Iraq's proposal to end the war, rejected by the Iranian government because 'the survival of their regime depended on the war' (p.116). Marji smokes a cigarette, stolen from her uncle, sealing her 'act of rebellion' against her mother's 'dictatorship' and farewelling her childhood (p.117).*

Marji's difficult rite of passage is not only political but also personal. She is eager to leave childhood behind, which means breaking the rules with older friends (p.111). Rebellion against parental authority is also a familiar adolescent rite of passage and Marji casts her mother as the 'dictator' she must oppose. For Marji, the political and the personal are often merged. Smoking the cigarette is also symbolic; it is a difficult initiation ritual to enter a seemingly sophisticated adult world.

Key point

The Iranian government's sacrifice of its people for political gain is unequivocally condemned. The large frame of a violent battle scene makes a strong point about the avoidable loss of a million lives (p.116).

The passport (pp.118–25)

Summary: *Marji's Uncle Taher considers the government's human rights abuses a 'bigger issue than the war' (p.118). Smoking heavily to cope with the stress of constant gunfire, he yearns to see his son, who is unable to return from abroad because of Iran's border closures. When a grenade is thrown outside his home, Taher suffers his third heart attack; he is taken to hospital where doctors cannot perform the open-heart surgery he needs. Obtaining a passport to go to England for surgery is difficult and Marji's father tries to organise a forged passport. The attempt fails when Niloufar, who helps the forger (Khosro), is arrested and executed, and Khosro flees. Taher dies without seeing his son.*

The enormous pressure on ordinary people, caused by war and government atrocities, is highlighted by Taher, who endangers his health with excessive smoking. Outside the hospital, the 'red crescent' trucks collect donations of blood for wounded soldiers – another indication of the vast numbers of war casualties, and of the government's expectation that citizens will shed blood for their country. The hospital bureaucrats don't provide the necessary permission for Taher's passport, citing God's will and higher wartime priorities. Khosro's thriving passport forgery business reveals people's desperation to leave Iran.

Key point

The shocking immorality of war is exposed through the doctor's revelation that the Germans sell chemical weapons to Iraq and Iran and the wounded soldiers are used as 'human guinea pigs' (p.122) when they are sent to Germany for medical treatment.

Kim Wilde (pp.126–34)

Summary: *In 1983 Iran's borders are reopened and Marji's parents travel to Turkey, promising to buy her a denim jacket and posters of Kim Wilde and Iron Maiden; they smuggle these banned Western goods into Iran. Marji wears her denim jacket and a Michael Jackson badge in the street, attracting attention from female members of the dreaded Guardians of the Revolution. They threaten to report her to the 'committee' but Marji lies to gain their sympathy and they let her go (p.134).*

Marji is strongly attracted to teen pop culture – in particular, the heavy metal band Iron Maiden and musician Kim Wilde, whose song 'Kids in America' celebrates the freedom of young people to enjoy themselves. Wearing symbols of Western decadence in the street, Marji is threatened with arrest by female Guardians; her terror is real, although the story about her cruel stepmother is comically excessive. It is not surprising that repressed teenagers like Marji are so strongly drawn to Western symbols of freedom.

Key point

Given her parents' willingness to break the rules by attending demonstrations and smuggling banned items into Iran, it is not surprising that Marji also crosses boundaries. Unlike her parents, however, Marji has not learned to be careful.

Q Are Marji's parents irresponsible in giving her illegal merchandise which could get her into serious trouble?

The Shabbat (pp.135–42)

Summary: *Tehran is heavily bombed by Iraq and Marji's neighbours, the Baba-Levys, are killed. When Marji and Taji walk past the rubble that was once their neighbours' house, Marji is horrified to see a turquoise bracelet belonging to Neda, the Baba-Levys' fourteen-year-old daughter, which is on her arm protruding from the rubble. Marji is overwhelmed by sorrow and anger.*

Marji and a friend are shopping when they hear that a missile has exploded in Marji's neighbourhood. Suddenly, the war has become much more dangerous for her, and Marji rushes home to see if her parents are safe. Her mother reassures her and says that, although the Baba-Levys' house was hit, they would not have been home; but, even before she sees the bracelet, Marji guesses the awful truth. Her distressed reaction to Neda's arm shows Marji's awareness that it could easily have been her own arm and her own family.

Key point

Marji's privileged lifestyle is reflected in the shopping expedition for jeans and jewellery: unnecessary luxuries in a war-torn country where food is sometimes scarce on supermarket shelves. The explosion of the bomb shows her how vulnerable their family is, despite her privilege.

Key vocabulary

Ballistic missile: a weapon that is shot through the air and is capable of travelling a great distance; when it reaches its target it explodes.

Scuds: long-range surface-to-surface guided missiles, able to be fired from mobile launchers.

The dowry (pp.143–53)

Summary: *At school, when the Principal tries to remove Marji's bracelet, Marji hits her and is expelled. Her parents find her another school, where she accuses the teacher of lying to the class. The other students applaud and the teacher phones Marji's parents, who begin to worry that she will be arrested, raped and executed, as Niloufar was. They decide to send her to Vienna. Marji's grandmother comes to stay and promises to visit her. At the airport, Marji's mother faints after saying goodbye to her, and is carried away by her father.*

The deaths of the Baba-Levys make Marji more rebellious because nothing scares her anymore (p.143). Yet her parents know what happens to virgins who are arrested. Because it is a crime to kill virgins, the girls are 'married' to one of the Guardians of the Revolution, who rapes them before they are executed (p.145). Marji is horrified, not only by the fate of young women like Niloufar, but by her own dangerous ignorance.

Key point

The separation of Marji from her family is a tragic consequence of a bitter conflict. On her last night at home, Marji nestles against her grandmother and tells herself she will never forget the smell of her bosom. This strong sensory imagery of maternal nurturing is a poignant reminder of the importance of family.

Key vocabulary

Dowry: money or property given by a bride's family to her bridegroom or his family when she marries.

Q What differences in Marji and her family can you identify if you compare this chapter to the first chapter?

CHARACTERS & RELATIONSHIPS

Marji / Marjane

Key quotes

'As for me, I love the King, he was chosen by God.' (p.19)

'... if women's hair got men excited, the same thing could be said of men's bare arms. And so, wearing short-sleeved shirts was also forbidden. There was a kind of justice after all.' (p.75)

'I will always be true to myself.' (p.151)

As a ten-year-old, Marji is a passionate and intelligent child who believes that she has been chosen by God to become a prophet. When the Shah is deposed and she is forced to wear the veil, she wants to join her parents at political demonstrations. As she tries to understand the politically complex world around her, Marji is guided by her father, with whom she has a strong and loving relationship. He tells her about Iran's history and recounts their own family's illustrious and heroic story, which gives her a stronger sense of who she is. He also refutes the lies she is told at school or hears on television. This helps her to define her moral and political values, which are strongly centred on social justice. Marji's relationship with her mother, Taji, is sometimes less affectionate, although Taji is as loving as Ebi. Taji is more of a disciplinarian, punishing Marji and Mehri harshly for attending the dangerous Black Friday demonstration (p.39).

As an adolescent, Marji's acts of rebellion increase, occurring at home, at school and in public. This is partly because of her social conscience, but also because she is a teenager who needs to express her individuality. She defiantly aligns herself with Western youth culture, publicly wearing clothing banned in Islamic Iran. In challenging the repressive dress code at one school, and exposing a teacher's lie at another, Marji's reveals her ignorance about what happens to dissenters. To avoid a fate like Niloufar's, Marji's parents decide she must leave Iran. She is heartbroken at leaving her home and family for the safety of a foreign country, but in Islamic Iran there is no other option for an intelligent young girl who is driven not only by a need for justice but also by a desire for education and a career.

The voice of the adult narrator often comments on the child's view of the world. Marjane's adult voice is often tolerant and amused, a quality evident, for instance, when she comments on Marji's certainty that she is 'the last prophet' (p.6). Satrapi's illustration gently mocks the naive six-year-old, whose head is drawn surrounded by the rays of the sun. Marji's voice becomes sadder and wiser as her view of the world changes. At the age of ten her dream is more grounded; she wants to be like Marie Curie, 'an educated, liberated woman' (p.73), but she knows that in the Islamic Republic this is impossible.

Mrs Satrapi (Taji)

Key quotes

'... it is not for you and me to do justice. I'd even say we have to learn to forgive.' (p.46)

'Our country has always known war and martyrs. So, like my father said: "when a big wave comes, lower your head and let it pass!"' (p.94)

Taji is a politically active woman, a loving wife and a caring mother. She opposes the corrupt, totalitarian regime of the Shah and, like many other Iranian women accustomed to freedom of choice, she publicly demonstrates against the enforcement of sharia law under the Islamic Republic. She is the daughter of a prince but her family was plunged into poverty when the first Shah took all their property. Although her father became prime minister, Taji lived in constant fear that he would be imprisoned for being a communist – which he frequently was, and it destroyed his health.

Taji is a passionate woman; her defiance of the veil is about defending women's 'freedom' (p.5). When her failure to wear a veil in the street results in a vicious verbal assault by the Guardians of the Revolution, she becomes ill and withdrawn, and fearful of being raped. Yet she still supports her daughter's defiance by buying banned Western clothing for her. Given Taji's own terrifying experience with the Guardians, this seems irresponsible, but also indicates her recognition of Marji's need for self-expression. Eventually, both mother and daughter conform to strict dress codes. Readers gain a sense of how ruthless and repressive the fundamentalist regime is through Marji and Taji's adoption of modesty codes, and through Taji's advice to her daughter: that, if asked, she should say that she prays all day (p.75).

Taji is also a protective mother, comforting Marji when she is overwhelmed by death and destruction, by repeating her father's words to 'lower your head and let it pass' (p.94). She guides her impetuous daughter along the path of forgiveness when Marji wants to torture Ramin because his father is in the secret police (p.45), yet she herself 'wanted to kill' those who torture others (p.52), and she tells Marji that evil-doers 'will pay for what they have done' (p.53). Taji's inconsistency highlights the blurred line between justice and vengeance in Iran – with its changing political landscapes. Taji's strict parenting of teenage Marji reflects her anxiety for her daughter's safety, and her grief at the airport when she farewells Marji reveals the deep love she has always had for her only child.

Mr Satrapi (Ebi)

Key quotes

'... in this country you must stay within your own social class.' (p.37)

'You can't always believe what they say ... The BBC is broadcasting too. Where's the radio?' (p.83)

'How can you be insensitive to the woman you love?' (to Taji, p.119)

Ebi is a loving and protective husband and father. The deep affection between him and his daughter is evident in illustrations of Marji on his lap as he tells her stories (p.19), or in his arms as he comforts or reassures her (p.30, p.68, pp.84–5, p.88, p.152). Ebi and Taji also have a strong relationship: she feels 'lucky' to be married to 'the kindest man on earth (p.119). Ebi's kindness encompasses his friends and extended family, as shown, for example, through his attempt to buy a forged passport for Uncle Taher's trip to England for life-saving surgery (p.123). Yet Marji is critical of her father's apparent lack of patriotism (p.83) and is disappointed that he is 'not a hero' (p.54). His courage, however, is evident when he takes photographs at demonstrations. This is 'strictly forbidden' and Ebi risks arrest and torture (p.29).

Ebi is also politically astute. 'It's incredible', he tells Anoosh, that 'the revolution is a leftist revolution and the republic wants to be called Islamic' (p.62). Marji learns a great deal by listening to 'political discussions of the highest order' between Anoosh and Ebi (p.62). She is disappointed and confused, however, by her socialist father's disapproval of Mehri's relationship with Hossein, based on their class differences. Yet when Hossein discovers Mehri's low social status, his hasty termination of the relationship confirms Ebi's judgement that 'in this country' their love was truly 'impossible' (p.37). As Marji later discovers, her father is a wise man who is usually 'right' (p.84).

Uncle Anoosh

Key quotes

'After the separation, I felt very lonely. I missed my country, my parents, my brothers. I dreamt about them often.' (p.60)

'Everything will be alright!' (p.65)

As a young man, Anoosh's rebellion against the Shah's oppression propels him into a separatist revolt in Azerbaijan, with his uncle, Fereydoon. When the revolution fails, he escapes to Russia where he marries a Russian girl and has two daughters. There is a shadow over Anoosh's relationship with his wife, suggested by his weeping when showing Marji a photograph with his wife's defaced image. He explains to Marji that his wife has no heart (p.59). The details of his failed marriage are never clarified and it is obviously a painful subject. Overwhelmed by homesickness in Russia, he returns to Iran in disguise, but is recognised, imprisoned and tortured relentlessly.

After his release from prison, Anoosh visits his nephew, Ebi. Marji immediately worships him as a patriot and a hero, and he returns her affection. Anoosh tries to remain optimistic about the possibility of proletarian rule (p.69), despite his communist friends being persecuted, imprisoned and executed. Before he himself is executed, he asks to see Marji, whom he regards as 'the little girl [he] always wanted to have' (p.69). Anoosh's tragic life is interwoven with Iran's bloody history of revolution and counter-revolution, the displacement of people and the disintegration of families.

Marji's grandmother

Key quotes

'To survive I took in sewing and with the leftover material, I made clothes for the whole family.' (p.27)

'... there is nothing worse than bitterness and vengeance ... Always keep your dignity and be true to yourself.' (p.150)

A strong, resourceful woman, Taji's mother and Marji's grandmother is a loving and comforting presence in Marji's life. She is also a proud woman, disguising her family's poverty from the neighbours by boiling water on the stove for dinner when they have no food (p.26). Many years after her husband's death, she still finds it painful to talk about his suffering, showing the strength and endurance of her love. Marji also draws on the strength of her grandmother's love the night before she leaves for Vienna as she rests her head against her grandmother's jasmine-scented breasts, listening to her words of encouragement. Her grandmother tells Marji to remain 'true' to herself and promises to visit Marji in Vienna. As Marji and her grandmother don't know when – if ever – they will see each other again, it is a sad parting for them both.

Uncle Taher

Key quotes

'The butcher told me he's seen kids executed in the street without even having been judged. The shame of it.' (p.118)

I have only one wish, and that's to see my son again, one last time.' (p.124)

Uncle Taher symbolises the older generation of ordinary Iranians. His family has been broken apart by the ongoing conflict and his health has been destroyed by anxiety. He smokes excessively and, after a third heart attack, he is rushed to the hospital, where there is no medical equipment to save him. Taher's application for a passport to England for life-saving surgery is delayed by bureaucracy and it is only his family connection with the Satrapis that offers him any hope. Ebi tries to buy Taher a forged passport. The attempt fails and Taher dies. Ironically, his legal passport arrives the day he is buried.

Mehri

Key quotes

'She was eight years old when she had to leave her parents' home to come to work for us' (p.34)

'Long live the republic!' (p.39)

It is significant that Mehri has almost no dialogue; she is representative of her class and gender in being denied a voice in a repressive patriarchal society. Unable to read or write, she relies on Marji to express her feelings for Hossein – the neighbours' son. She attends the Black Friday demonstration with Marji but it is not clear that she understands its political agenda. Mehri is typical of young girls of her class; bound by her servitude to a wealthy family, she will have limited opportunities for marriage and a family of her own. One of Mehri's few utterances is 'long live the republic' (p.39); Ironically, the Islamic Republic will deny both Mehri and Marji opportunities for education and liberty.

Siamak

Key quote

> '... when they arrested me, Laly barely spoke and now she is a real young lady.' (p.49)

Siamak, like many other idealistic young men, is imprisoned and tortured during the Shah's regime and released after the Shah's fall, only to find himself in opposition to another oppressive anti-communist regime. He is hunted by Islamic fundamentalists, who murder his sister when they cannot find him. Siamak and his family escape from Iran by crossing the border, hidden among a flock of sheep. The sheep – some of them likely destined for slaughter – are symbolic of the family's powerlessness.

Laly

Key quote

> '... my father is a hero!' (p.52)

Laly and her mother visit the Satrapis after Siamak has been missing for ten months. Laly has been told that he is 'on a trip' (p.48) which, as Marji knows, is usually a euphemism to mean that someone is dead. She tells Laly this and is sent to her room for upsetting Laly. When Siamak is released and visits the Satrapis, Laly, still angry with Marji, refuses to play with her. Marji's attempt to justify her previous inappropriate honesty is rebuffed by Laly, whose comment that her father is 'a hero' (p.52) implies a moral failure in Marji's family. Laly's lack of forgiveness shows how deeply upset she was by Marji's insensitivity. In turn, Marji is strongly affected by Laly's words, as shown visually in the frame on page 52 where Laly suddenly becomes twice Marji's size, towering significantly over her.

Mrs Jari

Key quote

> 'No, no … of course he's not.' (Reassuring Laly that her father is not dead, p.48)

Apart from denying Marji's assertion that Siamak is dead, Mrs Jari has no other dialogue, nor even a first name. She has background conversations with Taji but takes no part in other interactions. By contrast, most other female characters are assertive and outspoken.

Mohsen

Key quote

> 'Me dead? What a joke! In prison they called me the man with seven lives.' (p.50)

Mohsen was acquainted with Siamak during their imprisonment. Visiting the Satrapis, he is reunited with Siamak and they describe in detail the horrific torture they endured. Mohsen reveals that the torturers were trained by the CIA (p.50). The enormous capacity for cruelty of totalitarian regimes, and even of democracies like the United States, is shocking. Also evident is the courage of people like Siamak and Mohsen. Their commitment to their cause is shown by their capacity to endure such torture. Mohsen's joke about his ability to survive proves to be ironic, as he is soon to be drowned in his bathtub by Islamic fundamentalists.

Mali, her husband and their two sons

Key quote

> 'To have the Iraqis attack, and to lose in an instant everything you had built over a lifetime, that's one thing … But to be spat upon by your own kind, it is intolerable!' (p.93)

After Iraq bombs the oil refinery at Abadan, Taji's childhood friend Mali and her family come to stay because their luxury home in Abadan is destroyed. Mali's 'materialistic' husband is upset about losing everything (p.90) and the two young boys act like 'brats' (p.92). At the supermarket,

Mali is upset by local women who blame refugees from bombed cities for Tehran's supermarket food shortages. The local women also accuse refugee women of prostituting themselves and Mali is deeply upset by this slur. Her dignity and honour mean more to Mali than the luxury of her former life. Unlike her husband and her sons, she is not materialistic.

Niloufar

Key quotes

'500 tumans for the life and virginity of an innocent girl.' (Taji, p.146)

'Niloufar was a real martyr, and her blood certainly did not feed our society's veins.' (Marji, p.146)

An eighteen-year-old girl who works for Khosro, the passport forger, Niloufar is another female character with no dialogue. She lives in Khosro's basement because the police are searching for her. She is eventually caught and executed for being a communist, and Marji's parents tell her Niloufar's tragic story. Because she is a virgin, and thus cannot legally be killed, Niloufar is 'married' to a Guardian of the Revolution, who takes her virginity before executing her. Hearing this, Marji reflects on the government's absurd political propaganda about the deaths of 'martyrs' – young men who die on the battlefield, and whose blood is said to be a life-giving transfusion for society. Marji sees Niloufar as a 'true hero' but Niloufar's female blood (and communist ideology) would disqualify her from being sacred or heroic under the regime. As a female and a communist sympathiser herself, Marji redefines martyrdom for herself so that it can encompass Niloufar's sacrifice.

Mrs Nasrine

Key quote

'They gave this to my son at school. They told the boys that if they went to war and were lucky enough to die, this key would get them into heaven.' (p.99)

Mrs Nasrine is the Satrapis' maid; she and her son are representative of society's lowest classes. When Mrs Nasrine's fourteen-year-old son receives a 'golden key', his mother, who has 'suffered so much' raising five children, is distraught that the government wants to 'trade' the key for her 'oldest son' (p.99). She feels bitter because she has been 'faithful to the religion' all her life, and finds it hard to 'believe in anything anymore' (p.99). The boy is excited by the promise of 'food, women and houses made of gold and diamonds' (p.100), and doesn't listen when Taji tells him that the government has fed him 'made-up stories' (p.100). The government takes advantage of the poverty and gullibility of these young boys and the powerlessness of their parents.

The Baba-Levys

Key quote

> 'Saturday is the Jewish Sabbath. Wherever they are, Jews are supposed to go home.' (p.141)

The Satrapis' neighbours are victims of circumstance when their house is demolished by a random air strike on Tehran. It is a tragic irony that these Jews who usually 'weren't very observant' of their faith are at home on the Sabbath (p.141). Marji identifies strongly with Neda, the quiet fourteen-year-old, with whom she sometimes chatted about romance (p.137). Marji's horror at discovering Neda's turquoise bracelet on the arm protruding from the rubble reveals her sorrow at the loss of an innocent life, and her sudden awareness of her own family's vulnerability. The final frame in this chapter (p.142) is solid black, signifying an overwhelming sense of despair and the nearness of death.

THEMES, IDEAS & VALUES

Identity

Key quotes

'Don't you think I look like Che Guevara?' (p.16)

'Misery! At the age that Marie Curie first went to France to study, I'll probably have ten children ...' (p.73)

'With this first cigarette, I kissed childhood goodbye. Now I was a grown-up.' (p.117)

Identity is the motif around which Satrapi's memoir is structured, as Marji searches for a sense of self against a backdrop of violence and repression. Six-year-old Marji is strong-minded and intelligent. She sees herself as a future prophet, speaking words of wisdom and championing social justice (p.6). As she matures, Marji's identity is shaped more by her rebelliousness against oppression than by her religious faith. She dresses up as Che Guevara (p.10) and wants to demonstrate against the Shah with her parents (p.17). Marji also values social equality: she reads about Marxism (p.12) and encourages her family's maid's relationship with the son of a wealthy neighbour (pp.36–7). She is an outspoken girl whose firm belief in the 'truth' gets her into trouble both at home (when she tells Laly her father is dead, p.48) and at school (when she calls the teacher a liar, p.144).

As a teenager, Marji is a rebel – undergoing a familiar rite of passage in her transition from childhood to adolescence. Like many teenagers, she connects strongly with a youth culture in which fashion and music are markers of identity. She wears banned denim clothing, and likes Kim Wilde and Iron Maiden, attracted by their celebration of freedom and rebelliousness (p.126). Marji's own adolescent rebelliousness leads her to skip class and hang out with friends at a cafe (p.112). She defies her mother's authority as well, referring to her as a 'dictator' (p.113). Yet Marji's family is important to her. As she prepares to leave for Vienna,

Marji is deeply saddened, especially as she may not see her beloved grandmother again. While Marji's uncompromising nature shows a degree of naivety, she also has a great deal of courage. Readers are positioned to endorse her values and admire her tenacity as she finds ways of remaining true to herself.

Other characters' identities are also shaped by their belief in the values of freedom, truth and justice. Taji is strongly defined by her opposition to both the Shah and the Islamic regime. She attends demonstrations (p.38, p.76) and is outspoken about gender inequality, encouraging Marji to 'defend her rights as a woman' (p.76). As a mother she is a harsh disciplinarian when Marji breaks the rules (p.39, p.113), but is protective as well, threatening to 'kill' anyone 'who touches a hair of [Marji's] head' (p.145). Taji's emotional collapse as Marji leaves for Vienna (p.153) emphasises the deeply loving and maternal side of her character.

Ebi's identity is very much connected to his paternal role, educating Marji about her historical and familial background (pp.19–23), and guiding her political views towards the need for 'truth' (p.62). His identity is also shaped by his role as a courageous and generous friend, endangering himself by helping others in need, such as Uncle Taher, who needs a forged passport (p.121).

Another uncle, Anoosh, embodies the identity of heroism in Marji's eyes for his involvement in revolution, and for the torture he endures in prison (pp.54–61). He is a strong and charismatic figure, yet constant separations from family surround him with an aura of sorrow.

Key point

The identities of the key characters in *Persepolis* are predominantly shaped by their moral values and political beliefs, and their unwavering commitment to family relationships.

Religion and politics

Key quotes

'We didn't really like to wear the veil, especially since we didn't understand why we had to.' (p.3)

'God is with us Reza, God is with us.' (a soldier, p.19)

'All my life, I've been faithful to the religion. If it's come to this... well, I can't believe anything anymore...' (Mrs Nasrine, p.99)

The first shah of Iran, a low-ranked soldier, overthrows the Emperor, believing that he is carrying out 'God's will' (p.19). Children are taught at school that the second shah was 'chosen by God' (p.19). The second shah is a secular Muslim and, while he rules, Islam coexists with remnants of Zarathustrianism, an ancient religion which values freedom of thought and expression. After the Islamic revolution, joyful Zarathustrian holidays like the 'Fire Ceremony' cease (p.7), but the loss of freedom of thought and expression in the new regime is more serious. In a theocracy (a government in which God is the highest leader), the amalgamation of religion and politics results in total control of the people by the government. Sharia law, as interpreted from passages in the Quran, is rigorously imposed in the new Iranian theocracy. Wearing the veil, for example, is part of a 'modesty' code which is strictly enforced by Guardians of the Revolution. Taji is threated with rape by 'bearded ... fundamentalists' (p.74) because her hair is uncovered. Marji is threatened with arrest by Guardians of the Revolution for wearing 'symbol[s] of decadence' (p.133), and could be detained by the 'Committee ... for hours' and 'whipped' (p.134).

In the Islamic Republic, praying is a sign of compliance with sharia law, and children are directed by anxious parents to lie at school about how many times a day they pray (p.75). Education is government-controlled and schools are places where children are indoctrinated. Loudspeakers churn out patriotic songs praising Iran's war effort and students are compelled to beat their breasts (p.96). Through this painful religious 'ritual', students symbolically share the suffering of Iranian soldiers in the battle against Iraq; when their parents object, they are told that students either 'obey the law' or 'they're expelled' (p.98). For Marji and her friends, their school day consists of knitting 'winter hoods for the soldiers' (p.97), covering themselves 'from head to toe' and being 'forbidden to play' (p.98). The continuation of the long war with Iraq is justified on religious grounds, as a need to capture the 'holy city' of Karbala (p.115) and the term 'martyr' is used to describe dead soldiers in a wilfully misleading manner: unlike many of the soldiers, martyrs willingly sacrifice their lives for their religious or moral beliefs.

Religion and politics infiltrate every aspect of people's lives. As people become more fearful, they comply more fully with sharia law. Some report their neighbours for suspected breaches. One neighbour, punished for 'planning a party', is sentenced to 'seventy-five lashes' and damaged so badly that he can no longer walk (p.105). It is little wonder that people become excessively compliant. This religiously sanctioned cruelty, Satrapi suggests, is totalitarian control at its worst. The sacrifice of young men, given golden keys to enter paradise should they die in battle, is even more ruthless. Mrs Nasrine, whose son is given a key, has been 'faithful' to religion and declares in miserable bewilderment: 'If it's come to this ... I can't believe in anything anymore' (p.99). Significantly, it is only the sons of the poor who are given these keys; if the government believed its own propaganda, wouldn't it want to help wealthier young men to reach paradise, too? Marji's cousin Sahab, a soldier himself, explains that 'first they convince them that the afterlife is even better than Disneyland ... They hypnotize them and just toss them into battle. Absolute carnage' (p.101).

Religion, Satrapi suggests, is utilised by the Islamic Republic to justify its extremism.

Gender

Key quotes

'You'll see. Soon they're actually going to force us to wear the veil ...' (Taji, p.73)

'Two fundamentalist bastards ... they said that women like me should be pushed up against a wall and fucked. And then thrown in the garbage.' (Taji, p.74)

'She should start learning to defend her rights as a woman right now!' (Taji, p.76)

Gender and politics converge in the Islamic Republic to empower men and discriminate against women. Iran is a patriarchal society where male gods, prophets and rulers preside over the political and social hierarchy. Heroism is almost exclusively defined as masculine and epitomised by Anoosh. Marji is overjoyed to have a 'hero' in her family (p.54). Anoosh is loyal, courageous and morally upright. More heroic, in Anoosh's eyes, is Uncle Fereydoon who tries to establish a republic in Azerbaijan and stoically submits to execution when he fails. Also portrayed as heroes are the men who die in battle, including Pardisse's father (p.86); and Siamak and Mohsen, who survive imprisonment and torture (p.47). Marji perceives heroism in terms of men's suffering and death and is disappointed that her father is 'not a hero' (p.54). Through Marji's narrative perspective, readers perceive how closely masculinity and heroism are combined in a patriarchal society.

Yet while she honours these heroic men, Marji also honours female revolutionary 'F. Rezaï' (p.12) and, by defining Niloufar as 'a real martyr' (p.146), claims a place for women in the ranks of heroes. Marji also challenges traditional gender expectations through her decision to become a 'prophet' (p.6), and through her desire to emulate Marie Curie. Like Marie Curie, Marji is prepared to sacrifice herself, even 'if the pursuit of knowledge meant getting cancer' (p.73). This kind of sacrifice is heroic as well, but does not demand blood and death on a battlefield or in prison and thus is not valued by the fundamentalist society.

Marji realises the political limitations of being female and, as a ten-year-old, symbolically crosses the gender divide by dressing up as Che Guevara to challenge the unjust rule of the Shah (p.10). After the Shah is deposed, Marji's political activism intensifies as the Islamic Republic becomes more repressive. Inspired by her mother, Marji demonstrates against the veil (p.76), following her mother's lead. Taji's opposition to the veil puts her in great danger when two Guardians of the Revolution threaten to rape her and throw her in the garbage (p.74). Their views of women as inferior beings, who can be sexually abused and discarded, indicate a deep misogyny embedded in patriarchal ideology. The debasement of women is also evident in the promise of plenty of 'food, women and houses made of gold' (p.100) made to young men to lure then into the army.

Despite Marji's objections, wearing the veil becomes necessary, as not wearing it will result in her expulsion from school (p.98). Ebi challenges Marji's teacher by suggesting that if hair is so 'stimulating' she should shave her 'moustache' (p.98). While this is amusing, Ebi is alluding to the injustice of making women responsible for men's sexual conduct by insisting that women cover themselves. Ebi also displays support for women's rights in illegally photographing demonstrators (p.29), and attending demonstrations against the veil (p.76). In her presentation of these assertive and resolute characters, Satrapi condemns the injustice of judging women solely by their sexuality, and mocks the absurdity of the notion that their hair is irresistibly erotic.

Key point

By showing how Marji challenges discrimination against women, Satrapi strongly positions readers to recognise the need to fight for social justice and equality in the Islamic Republic.

Truth, lies and propaganda

Key quotes

'The BBC said there were 400 victims. The Shah said that a group of religious fanatics perpetrated the massacre. But the people knew that it was the Shah's fault!!!' (p.15)

'The elections were faked and they believe the results: 99.99%!! As for me, I don't know a single person who voted for the Islamic Republic. Where did that figure come from?' (Ebi, p.62)

'The walls were suddenly covered with belligerent slogans ... The one that struck me most by its gory imagery was: "To die a martyr is to inject blood into the veins of society."' (p.115)

Marji begins to understand the difference between fact and propaganda when her father's account of historical events reveals that the King (Shah) was not chosen by God, as is written in her school book (p.19). She also begins to see how a lie might become a truth if it is repeated often and with sufficient conviction. Ebi's story about the crowd at the hospital, honouring as a martyr the old man who died of cancer, reinforces this notion. Even though the widow insists that her husband was not killed by the Shah, the angry crowd continues to proclaim him a hero, and she suddenly and enthusiastically joins in the chant that 'the King is a killer' (p.32). While her parents and grandmother find this highly amusing, Marji realises that she doesn't 'understand anything' (p.32), and searches for the truth in books.

Marji also discovers that the truth can be what people choose to believe, and this often depends on their political allegiances. After the tragic fire at the Rex Cinema, the Shah blames 'religious fanatics' but the people, with their hatred of the Shah, 'knew' that it was 'the Shah's fault' (p.1). After the fall of the Shah, 'strange phenomena' occur: for example, Marji's neighbours allege that a mark on the cheek of the neighbour's wife is the result of a bullet wound received in a demonstration against the Shah (p.44). The Satrapis know that 'she always had that nasty spot' (p.44), but the neighbours want to believe, and want others to believe, their story. When a lie is unchallenged, as this one is, it passes for the truth. Ebi regards it as 'not important' to expose the lie (p.44), but there are times when it is. When the news about Iran's bombing of Baghdad is broadcast by the Islamic regime, Ebi needs to check with the BBC (p.83), an independent and reliable source of 'truth'.

Like her father, Marji believes that truth is important but her attempt to enlighten Laly, by telling her that her father is probably dead, is misguided. Marji reflects that 'the truth is sometimes hard to accept' (p.48), assuming she is correct, but when Siamak returns, Marji realises that evidence based on probability is no guarantee of the truth. At school Marji is punished for questioning the teacher, whose order to the children to tear pictures of the Shah out of their schoolbooks contradicts a previous 'truth': that the Shah was 'chosen by God' (p.44). For Marji, the difference between truth and lies is often confusing, as is knowing when to speak out and when to remain silent. As well as sometimes being contradicted, facts are also sometimes invented in the new Islamic Republic. Listening to Anoosh and her father discuss politics, Marji informs them that '99% of the population voted for the Islamic Republic', but Ebi argues that 'the elections were faked' (p.62).

When the war with Iraq begins, government propaganda intensifies. Slogans cover the walls (p.115) and soldiers killed in battle are 'martyrs' (p.94). Public mourning in the form of self-flagellation becomes obligatory in schools (p.96). Perhaps the most iniquitous propaganda, however, is the 'made-up stories' told to the sons of the poor, who are promised plenty of 'food, women and houses made of gold' in return for their martyrdom (p.100). Marji becomes adept at recognising propaganda. She calculates that, if the number of Iraqi planes and tanks the government claims to have destroyed were true, the Iraqi army must have had more equipment than the US military, which seems highly improbable.

Government propaganda also disguises the real reason for the unnecessarily long war. Iran rejects what it calls an 'imposed peace' suggested by Iraq, deliberately making the settlement sound like a disadvantage to Iran (p.114). The government then plunges the country 'deeper into war' by insisting on the capture of Karbala (p.115). Yet it is later revealed that the 'survival of the regime depended on the war', and the needless sacrifice of 'a million people' (p.116).

Key point

The manipulation of the truth by the government for its own political purposes is an inevitable consequence of its unassailable power. Throughout her memoir, Satrapi emphasises the importance of truth in a creating a just and peaceful society.

The importance of family

Key quotes

'I tell you all this because it's important that you know. Our family memory must not be lost.' (Anoosh, p.60)

'I have only one wish, and that's to see my son again, one last time.' (Taher, p.124)

'What I had feared was true. Maybe they'd come to visit, but we'd never live together again.' (p.152)

As the world is shattered by violence and tainted by fear, family becomes very important to people. Marji's parents encourage and protect her while still allowing her the independence she needs. They teach her about truth, justice and tolerance: Ebi exposes the falsehood she is told at school about the King being 'chosen by God' (p.19), and Taji guides her towards an understanding of 'justice' and forgiveness (p.46). Her parents stimulate her interest in politics through their active opposition to both the Shah (p.16) and the Islamic Republic (p.76). Taji is also a protective mother; she punishes Marji for disobeying her to attend a demonstration. Yet Taji breaks rules herself, risking harsh punishment when she smuggles illegal Western music and clothing from Turkey for Marji. This is an endorsement of Marji's rebellious and independent character, suggesting it is inherited from her mother (p.119).

Marji's grandmother also exemplifies the importance of family. She is an integral part of Marji's family, and the only one who believes in Marji's ability to become a prophet (p.8). As a young wife and mother, Marji's grandmother 'lived in poverty' when 'the Shah's father' seized all their possessions (p.26), and she 'took in sewing' to support her own family (p.27). Her husband was frequently imprisoned for being a communist (p.24) and she became adept at 'hiding his tracts' when the police knocked at the door (p.109). She is a strong and loving woman whose commitment to her family is unwavering.

Marji's uncles are another important representation of family in her world. Anoosh left the safety of Russia to return to his country and his family (p.60). When he is released from prison he is welcomed by the Satrapis and Marji becomes 'the little girl' he 'always wanted to have' (p.69). After Anoosh's arrest, the image of his empty chair at the dinner table emphasises the incompleteness of Marji's family without him (p.67). Taher's family is also torn apart by the war, with his son living in Holland for safety. Smoking excessively to cope with his son's absence, and stressed by the constant gunshots (p.118), Taher suffers a heart attack. Although endangering himself, Ebi helps his brother-in-law by trying to obtain a forged passport for Taher to have life-saving surgery in England. Taher's death partially caused by grief over his son, and Ebi's willingness to risk his own safety both reaffirm the importance of family – especially in times of crisis.

Another family tragically divided by political upheaval is Siamak's. The time he lost – Laly's precious childhood years – while he languished in prison during the Shah's regime is 'irretrievable' (p.49) and casts a shadow of sorrow over the family's reunion. Laly and her mother's fears for Siamak after his disappearance, and Pardisse's similar wish that her father was 'alive and in jail rather than dead and a hero' (p.86), highlight the importance of the family unit for the wellbeing of its members. Mrs Nasrine is another victim of the assault on families during successive totalitarian regimes. Weeping, she talks of how much she has 'suffered', raising her children with the 'water of [her] tears', and she bitterly resents the government's 'trade' of a plastic key for her oldest son (p.99). In a war-torn country, under an extremist totalitarian government, the fundamental importance of family is shown through those struggling to survive and remain together. For example, the desperate escape of Siamak and his family, hidden among a flock of sheep (p.66), emphasises their need to stay together. Ironically, in the end Marji's family is only able to survive by sending her to live abroad, where she is safe.

Stories

Key quotes

'Come sit on my lap. I'll try to explain it to you.' (Ebi, p.19)

'I bought you some books. You will see why the people are revolting.' (Marji's grandmother, p.28)

'Listen, child, those are just made-up stories! What hell? What paradise?' (p.100)

The stories told to Marji are important in showing her who she is and how she should live her life. Ebi's story about 'certain things' that Marji 'should know' (p.22) includes historical events in Iran, interwoven with significant events in her family history (pp.19–23). Ebi relates the story of how the Emperor (her great-grandfather) was overthrown by a soldier who became the first Shah (p.22). Her grandfather (a prince) became, firstly, the Shah's prime minister and later his political prisoner. As granddaughter of a prince Marji suddenly becomes part of a larger narrative – one about nobility and power, which greatly appeals to her fertile imagination. Like all stories, Ebi's also has an instructive purpose; he teaches Marji that what is 'written' in her 'schoolbook' is not always true (p.19).

Marji also finds that moral values are embedded in narratives. As the Shah's prime minister, Marji's grandfather reads Marx and Lenin and becomes aware of the social injustice he had been blind to as a prince. Marx's *Communist Manifesto* is the history (or 'story') of class struggles across the centuries and it radically alters the former prince's conservative values. Ironically, as a prime minister with a 'conscience', Marji's grandfather now lacks the power of a prince to facilitate social change (p.23). Marji's social conscience is awakened by reading Ashraf Darvishian's stories about poor children, forced to work to support their families, and she has a narrative that helps her understand why she feels 'ashamed' to sit in her father's Cadillac (p.33).

Taji's story about the water-cell torture inflicted on her father (the former prince) has a profound effect on Marji and she spends 'a very long time in the bath', emulating her grandfather's suffering (p.25). This illustrates the emotional power of stories to elicit empathy for those who suffer. Marji has a similarly emotional response to the dreadful stories of Siamak and Mohsen who were tortured in prison. In recounting these stories, the two men celebrate their survival, and honour the memory of Ahmadi, who 'suffered the worst torture' (p.51) and was finally 'cut to pieces' (p.52). Remembrance of the dead is central to narrative traditions, where the values of dead heroes are celebrated in order to inspire the living. Listening to Siamak and Mohsen, Marji is shocked – not just by the calculated cruelty of the CIA-trained torturers (p.50), but also that a household appliance (an ordinary iron) can become an instrument of torture (p.51). She now sees the enormous potential for cruelty in the everyday world and her dramatically altered perception illustrates the transformative power of narrative.

Another example of this is Anoosh's story of courage and hardship. Anoosh fulfils Marji's desire to have a hero in her family. His telling of his story, and Marji's hearing of it, forges a permanent bond between them. Through Satrapi's retelling, Anoosh's story becomes part of Marji's. Marji's connection to Anoosh is so strong that, after his death, she becomes entirely disconnected from her familiar world. She angrily orders God, her former 'friend' (p.53), to 'get out' of her life (p.70). In a world without Anoosh, she finds herself floating in a black void, and is 'lost, without any bearings' (p.71).

Key point

Marji's strong connection with stories leads her to become a writer herself, retelling the stories of her country and her family so that those like Anoosh, who 'lost their lives ... defending freedom ... who suffered under various repressive regimes, or who were forced to leave their families and flee their homeland', will not be 'forgotten' (Introduction to *Persepolis*). In this sense, *Persepolis* is a story about telling stories, and a recognition of the importance of stories in people's lives.

DIFFERENT INTERPRETATIONS

Different interpretations arise from different responses to a text. Over time, a text will evoke a wide range of responses from its readers, who may come from various social or cultural groups and live in very different places and historical periods. Responses by critics and reviewers can be published in newspapers, journals and books, both online and in print. They can also be expressed in discussions among readers in the media, classrooms, book groups and so on.

While there is no single correct reading or interpretation of a text, it is important to understand that an interpretation is more than a personal opinion – it is the justification of a point of view on the text. To present an interpretation of a text based on your point of view, you must use a logical argument and support it with relevant evidence from the text.

The critics' viewpoints

'God Looked Like Marx', a 2003 review by Fernanda Eberstadt in *The New York Times*, speaks to a sophisticated audience which, Eberstadt assumes, is familiar with postmodernism and Marxism. Many readers will strongly sympathise with the 'tough, sassy little Iranian girl' Eberstadt identifies, and with her concerns about Islamic fundamentalism. Eberstadt recognises Marji's desire for honesty in her need to pry from 'her evasive elders if not truth, at least a credible explanation of the travails they are living through'. Eberstadt also approves of Marji's Marxist sympathies, evident in her reference to Marji's visit to Mehri's bedroom to comfort her after her boyfriend dumps her. Marji's sharing of Mehri's bed is a symbolic erasure of the class boundaries that separate Mehri from her boyfriend.

Eberstadt invites sympathy for Marji and her schoolmates who are forced to wear the veil and are taught 'self-flagellation instead of algebra'. She focuses on Marji's courage, quoting her announcement in class that 'contrary to the teacher's lies, there are a hundred times as many political prisoners under the revolution than there were under the Shah'. She also notes Marji's awareness that 'it's the poor who suffer', when peasant boys her age are armed with plastic keys giving them entry to paradise if they die in battle. Readers from Western democracies are strongly positioned by Eberstadt's review to admire this young Iranian girl's courage, compassion and egalitarian values.

In Geoffrey Macnab's interview with Satrapi (2006), Macnab begins with a reference to the alarming incident involving two fundamentalist Iranian women (Guardians of the Revolution) who threaten to report teenage Marji for wearing symbols of Western decadence: sneakers, jeans, a baseball cap and, worst of all, a Michael Jackson badge. Macnab likes the unexpectedness of Satrapi's account of the political turmoil in Iran 'from the perspective of a young girl who loves Kim Wilde and Iron Maiden'. He describes Satrapi's narrative voice as 'different: brash, well-informed, full of political and pop cultural references'. Macnab also mentions Satrapi's humour, observing that 'the funniest bits often come at the darkest moments'. He quotes Satrapi, who believes that 'when you go through war and revolution, the only thing you can do is laugh. It's a way of surviving'. Macnab favourably compares Marji, the 'precocious little Marx-quoting nine-year-old', with the 'equally smart and self-righteous Lisa in *The Simpsons*'. The familiar American cultural references will appeal to young Western readers despite Marji's criticism of Western leaders such as George Bush who (exactly like the mullahs) believe that God is their country's 'best friend'.

In 2017, Emma Lawson reviewed *Persepolis* for the popular website *ComicsAlliance*. Visitors to the site reading the review are immediately confronted with a large black-and-white-movie frame, showing Marji cowering below two menacing veiled women. Satrapi's condemnation of the repressive Islamic regime is succinctly conveyed through the contrast between the black-clad women dominating the frame, and the white-clad figure of the small child. This image differs from the one in the graphic novel of the same incident and it strongly implies the moral values of the characters involved. Lawson begins with an overview of the political situation after the 1978–79 revolution, which included the imposition of 'gender segregation, the abolition of secular education, and the strict enforcement of sharia law'. Lawson articulates how Marji's denim jacket and purchase of illegal Western music symbolise her rebellion against the new regime and hints that adolescents who are rebels themselves will strongly identify with the protagonist. Lawson's review is a prelude to a 'coming of age ... mixtape' of musicians and songs mentioned in *Persepolis*. Songs include such heavy metal classics as 'Run to the Hills' by Iron Maiden (expressing the need for freedom of an oppressed people), and Kim Wilde's mainstream 'Kids in America', which represents 'the 'freedom of culture and freedom of expression' that Lawson observes Marji seeking in *Persepolis*.

Two interpretations

Interpretation 1

In *Persepolis,* Marjane Satrapi presents a pessimistic view of life under a totalitarian regime.

In Iran during Marjane Satrapi's childhood, totalitarian governments exert rigid control over people's lives. Public demonstrations against injustice and corruption under the Shah's rule are brutally suppressed by the police and in the Islamic Republic oppressive government control extends to all facets of people's lives. When sharia law is imposed, the amalgamation of religion and politics denies people freedom of expression. Islamic fundamentalist rulers interpret the Quran in ways that justify oppression, and government corruption makes life unbearable for those who value freedom, truth and justice. Under this regime, there is virtually no hope of ever achieving such things.

The loss of individual freedom in the Islamic Republic is apparent in the strict dress code, with a particular focus on the veil. The danger of not complying is shockingly illustrated by Taji's experience when two fundamentalists accost her in the street and assert that unveiled women should be raped and 'thrown in the garbage' (p.74). In order to avoid harassment, many women publicly display their allegiance to the regime by wearing the chador (p.75) and, as Taji predicted, the veil becomes 'obligatory' (p.74). As the government becomes more merciless people are terrified into submission and a pervasive pessimism spreads throughout the community; children are instructed by their parents to lie about how often they pray. News of the savage punishment inflicted on Tinoosh's father for 'planning a party' (p.105) and for possession of banned items spreads throughout the neighbourhood and serves as warning about the danger of breaking the rules. A more serious concern, however, is that he was reported by 'someone' in the neighbourhood (p.75). The subsequent erosion of trust between people leads Taji to drape black curtains over the windows.

As well as trust and freedom being eroded, truth is also jeopardised in a totalitarian regime. The lie about the Shah being 'chosen by God' (p.19) implicitly endorses the corruption of his regime. Lies also proliferate in the Islamic Republic: Mrs Nasrine's naive fourteen-year-old son believes the 'made-up story' about gold-painted plastic keys opening the gates of paradise – and when Taji tries to tell him the truth, he is more interested in eating cake (p.100). When many people continue to believe a lie, it begins to seem like truth, leading readers to doubt that actual truth can survive under such conditions. The widespread credibility of lies is shown in the illustration of 'thousands of young kids, promised a better life, exploded on the minefields with their keys around their necks' (p.102). As the war with Iraq intensifies, 'belligerent slogans' (p.115) cover the walls in Tehran glorifying as martyrs those killed in battle, while in reality the soldiers are needlessly slaughtered because 'the survival of the regime depended on the war' (p.116). Ebi's total cynicism regarding the government's truthfulness is shown through his constant need to verify the accuracy of the Iranian news by listening to the BBC (pp.83–4).

Further cause for despair is the absence of justice in the Islamic Republic. When Anoosh is accused of being a 'Russian spy' and executed (p.70), Marji remembers his futile hope that 'everything will be alright', despite the murder of Mohsen by the government because he is communist (p.65). With Anoosh's death, Marji's faith in God is shattered (p.70). When Niloufar is hunted down and executed for being a communist, and also raped so that her executioner does not kill a virgin, Marji's horror at the injustice of Niloufar's fate is coupled with bitter cynicism towards a government that paid the 'equivalent of $5.00' to Niloufar's parents for 'the life and virginity of an innocent girl' (p.146). Niloufar's execution is not only unjust but also evil, and Marji's parents despair that she can survive in a society where injustice is officially sanctioned. By sending Marji to live in Austria, her parents reveal their pessimism about the prospect of 'justice on earth' (p.53). Hope is eradicated by the ruthlessness of the Islamic regime in maintaining its grip on absolute power.

Marji's departure from her homeland, and the tearful parting from her family, end her memoir on a note of sorrow. Separated from her grieving parents 'behind the glass', she reflects that 'saying goodbye' is 'a little like dying' (p.153). This connection with death very powerfully emphasises a loss of hope, not only for freedom and justice, but also for survival under a corrupt totalitarian regime.

Interpretation 2

Despite the tragedies in people's lives, there are many moments of hope and humour in *Persepolis*.

Marjane Satrapi's memoir is an account of life under a corrupt totalitarian regime, firstly during the reign of the Shah and, more terribly, in the Islamic Republic. Yet, despite the constant danger and the many moments of despair, Satrapi shows how people manage to survive, finding ways to celebrate and to surreptitiously defy their ruthless authoritarian rulers. Satrapi portrays strong and courageous characters, and reveals the power of humour to nourish the human spirit.

Marji's determination to fight oppression shows her strength of spirit. As a young child, she dresses up as Che Guevara (p.10) and also pleads with her parents to take her to demonstrations against the Shah (p.17). As an adolescent, she openly challenges her teacher's 'lie' about the absence of political prisoners in the Islamic Republic, inspiring her classmates to applaud her courage (p.144). The triumph of truth over a lie keeps alive a faint hope that the truth will not always be suppressed. Further signs of optimism are the many covert acts of resistance in the community, showing people's resilience and courage. For example, 'in spite of all the dangers', parties are still held: one of them with 'gallons' of alcohol made in Marji's uncle's basement (p.106). It is not simply the parties, however, that make life 'psychologically bearable' (p.106); it is also the continued resistance of oppressed people, keeping alive the hope that the regime can be challenged, even if only in secret. The thriving black market, where Marji buys her illegal Kim Wilde tape (p.132), is clear a symbol of optimism in its subversive challenge to the terrifying power of the regime.

Humour is another sign of optimism; used as a weapon against despair, it is a recurring motif in the text. Satrapi's humour is often directed at the self-righteous child she once was. She invites readers to share her amusement at young Marji's inconsistency when she changes from being 'very religious' to declaring that her faith is 'not unshakeable' (p.10) and embracing her new attraction to Che Guevara's revolutionary ideals. This lightheartedness balances the tragic aspects of the text which might otherwise become overwhelming. Ebi's encounter with fundamentalist police, who suspect him of drinking alcohol, seems to be heading for catastrophe, but Satrapi turns it into a dark comedy with rising tension created by villainous police, alcohol frantically poured down the toilet, and a humorous anticlimax in Ebi's need for a reviving drink (pp.108–10).

There is also humour embedded in certain language choices. In the supermarket, Mali's two young sons laugh uncontrollably at Marji's comment about beans and flatulence (p.92). Their childish enjoyment of the word 'fart' softens the impact of the two local women's cruel comments about refugees. Satrapi's illustration emphasises this point as the complaining women in the background are visibly diminished by the laughing children and their mothers, who dominate the frame (p.92). Uttering vulgar words is liberating because it implicitly challenges society's rules. A sense of liberation is integral to this kind of humour, in its total lack of respect for rigid authoritarianism.

Mockery is another form of humour and is often used to undermine unjust authorities. When Marji and her school friends can no longer take the self-flagellating 'torture sessions' seriously, they begin 'making fun of them' (p.97). They mimic the 'martyrs' and beg to be killed, and use toilet paper as decoration for 'the anniversary of the revolution' (p.97). This blatant disrespect is a highly optimistic sign, as it indicates the failure of the government's attempt to indoctrinate students. Another positive sign is that the students are 'completely united' (p.97) in their refusal to be intimidated by the threat of punishment. Ebi is capable of mockery as well, suggesting that the teacher shave her 'mustache' (p.98). As the enforcer of the rules regarding coverage of women's hair, the teacher is accused by Ebi of disobeying them, but his mockery is really directed at the so-called 'stimulating' effects of women's hair – which is humorously exposed as being ridiculous (p.98). Marji's ironic comment about the 'justice' of making men cover their arms (p.75) is also designed to mock the absurdity of the Islamic regime's attitude to hair and the assumption that sexual desire cannot be controlled.

Marjane Satrapi creates strong characters in her memoir, and draws upon symbolism and humour, to show that resistance and subversiveness can challenge a powerful and unjust regime and perhaps, eventually, defeat it. Satrapi herself celebrates laughter, and has been quoted as saying that 'when you go through war and revolution, the only thing you can do is laugh. It's a way of surviving' and 'humour', she adds, 'is the most subversive weapon' (Macnab 2006).

QUESTIONS & ANSWERS

This section focuses on your own analytical writing on the text, and gives you strategies for producing high-quality responses in your coursework and exam essays.

Essay writing – an overview

An essay on a literary work is a formal and serious piece of writing that presents your point of view on the text, usually in response to a given topic. Your 'point of view' in an essay is your interpretation of the meaning of the text's language, structure, characters, situations and events, supported by detailed analysis of textual evidence.

Analyse – don't summarise

In your essays it is important to avoid simply summarising what happens in a text.

- A **summary** is a description or paraphrase (retelling in different words) of the characters and events. For example: 'Macbeth has a horrifying vision of a dagger dripping with blood before he goes to murder King Duncan.'
- An **analysis** is an explanation of the real meaning or significance that lies 'beneath' the text's words (and images, for a film). For example: 'Macbeth's vision of a bloody dagger shows how deeply uneasy he is about the violent act he is contemplating, and conveys his sense that supernatural forces are impelling him to act.'

A limited amount of summary is sometimes necessary to let your reader know which part of the text you wish to discuss. However, always keep this to a minimum and follow it immediately with your analysis of what this part of the text is really telling us.

Plan your essay

Carefully plan your essay so that you have a clear idea of what you are going to say. The plan ensures that your ideas flow logically, that your argument remains consistent and that you stay on the topic. An essay plan should be a list of **brief dot points** covering no more than half a page.

- Include your central argument or main contention – a concise statement of your overall response to the topic.
- Write three or four dot points for each paragraph, indicating the main idea and evidence/examples from the text. Note that in your essay you will need to *expand* on these points and *analyse* the evidence.

Structure your essay

An essay is a complete, self-contained piece of writing. It has a clear beginning (the introduction), middle (several body paragraphs) and end (the last paragraph or conclusion). It must also have a central argument that runs throughout, linking each paragraph to form a coherent whole. See examples of introductions and conclusions in the 'Analysing a sample topic' and 'Sample answer' sections.

The introduction establishes your overall response to the topic. It includes your main contention and outlines the main evidence you will refer to in the course of the essay. Write your introduction *after* you have done a plan and *before* you write the rest of the essay.

The body paragraphs argue your case – they present evidence from the text and explain how this evidence supports your argument. Each body paragraph needs:

- a strong **topic sentence** (usually the first sentence) that states the main point being made in the paragraph
- **evidence** from the text, including some brief quotations
- **analysis** of the textual evidence, with **explanation** of its significance and how it supports your argument
- **links back to the topic** in one or more statements, usually towards the end of the paragraph.

Connect the body paragraphs so that your discussion flows smoothly. Use some linking words and phrases such as 'similarly' and 'on the other hand', though don't start every paragraph like this. Another strategy is to use a significant word from the last sentence of one paragraph in the first sentence of the next.

Use key terms from the topic – or synonyms for them – throughout, so the relevance of your discussion to the topic is always clear.

The conclusion ties everything together and finishes the essay. It includes strong statements that emphasise your central argument and provide a clear response to the topic.

Avoid simply restating the points made earlier in the essay – this will end on a very flat note and imply that you have run out of ideas and vocabulary. The conclusion should be a logical extension of what you have written, not just a repetition or summary of it. Writing an effective conclusion can be a challenge. Try using these tips:

- Start by linking back to the final sentence of the second-last paragraph – this helps your writing to flow, rather than leaping back to your main contention straight away.
- Use synonyms and expressions with equivalent meanings to vary your vocabulary. This allows you to reinforce your line of argument without being repetitive.
- When planning your essay, think of one or two broad statements or observations about the text's wider meaning. These should be related to the topic and your overall argument. Keep them for the conclusion, since they will give you something 'new' to say but still follow logically from your discussion. The introduction will be focused on the topic, but the conclusion can present a wider view of the text.

Essay topics

1. Before Marji leaves Iran, Marji's grandmother advises her to "be true to yourself".
   Why is this so difficult for Marji in her journey from childhood to adolescence?
2. 'It is Satrapi's illustrations that so powerfully convey the central ideas in *Persepolis*.' Discuss.
3. '*Persepolis* shows us that the relentless pursuit of power will always have tragic consequences.' Do you agree?
4. 'The comic-book style of Satrapi's memoir detracts from the seriousness of the issues she explores.' To what extent do you agree?
5. What role does storytelling play in *Persepolis*?
6. '*Persepolis* shows us that, amid overwhelming violence and corruption, survival is the only thing that matters.' Discuss.
7. 'It is family relationships that hold people together in the fractured society of Iran.'
   How does Satrapi convey this idea in *Persepolis*?
8. 'In *Persepolis*, Satrapi shows us that to be a woman or to be poor in this society is to be powerless.' Discuss.
9. Marji says, "So my father was not a hero ... if only he had been in prison".
   What view of heroism is presented in *Persepolis*?
10. "Bad people are dangerous but forgiving them is too. Don't worry, there is justice on earth."
    How is the idea of justice explored in *Persepolis*?

Analysing a sample topic

'*Persepolis* shows us that, amid overwhelming violence and corruption, survival is the only thing that matters.' Discuss.

It is crucial to look closely at any key word in a topic, such as 'survival' here, and ask what is meant by it. In *Persepolis*, 'survival' clearly encompasses physical survival, but psychological survival is shown to be equally important. This topic makes a generalisation that must be interrogated by challenging the assertion that survival is 'the *only* thing' that matters. Always ask if the topic's assertion or its underlying assumptions are consistent with what the text shows us. The response developed below argues that in some cases, an individual's physical survival may *not* be the most important issue.

Sample introduction

> Iran during the rule of the Shah is a dangerous place, where government corruption is rife and opposition to the Shah is brutally punished. After he is overthrown, the even more repressive rule of the Islamic Republic makes life extremely dangerous as people struggle to survive, not only physically but also psychologically. In a society where freedom of thought and expression has been abolished and where rebellion is punishable by imprisonment or death, people often remain alive by making compromises. In some cases, their psychological wellbeing is destroyed, and many decide that compromise is too high a price to pay for survival.

Body paragraph outline

Paragraph 1:

- Under successive totalitarian regimes in *Persepolis*, many people willingly comply. Ramin and his father (a member of the secret police, p.44) support the Shah – they believe communists are 'evil' and should be killed (p.46). The Guardians of the Islamic Revolution not only comply but force others to do so, relishing their newly-acquired power; one example is the armed Guardians who threaten to search Ebi's house for alcohol (p.108). For such people, physical survival is paramount.

- Other people compromise their values (such as freedom, justice, equality) in order to survive, such as the Islamic woman who once wore miniskirts but now is fully covered by the chador (p.75). The betrayal of Tinoosh's father by neighbours shows fear of non-conformity destroys community relationships. Taji is emotionally scarred after the rape threat by fundamentalists (p.74); she wears the veil in order to survive. In an atmosphere of fear and suspicion, tyranny flourishes and the people suffer.
- Many people risk their lives to avoid making unacceptable compromises. Siamak's family escapes concealed among a flock of sheep (p.66). In such repressive regimes, individuals are forced to examine their values and decide whether their physical survival is worth more than their principles.

Paragraph 2:

- Acts of defiance show that defending one's freedom is of the utmost importance: the alcohol made in Marji's uncle's basement makes life 'psychologically bearable' (p.106); the black market (p.132) and Khosro's forgery business (p.123) demonstrate people's willingness to risk their liberty and their lives to enable their psychological survival.
- Demonstrations against the shah (p.18, pp.38–9) and the veil (p.76) suggest that physical survival is often less important than the erosion of values that results from silence and compliance.
- Marji's public challenge of a teacher's 'lie' (p.144) inspires other students to declare support; but Niloufar's fate shows the horrific consequences of non-conformity (p.146).

Paragraph 3:

- Marji's grandfather, Fereydoon, Anoosh, Mohsen, Siamak, Marji, Ebi and Taji all risk their lives and liberty – some die upholding values (freedom, justice equality).
- Marji is inspired by 'martyrs' killed by the Shah (p.12), but because of her outspokenness, her exile becomes necessary for her physical survival – this causes psychological damage to the entire family (pp.150–3).
- Those who die (such as Ahmadi, p.52 and Fereydoon, p.57) consider psychological survival (commitment to values) more important than physical survival.

Sample conclusion

> Given the choice between fighting for justice and being tortured or executed, it is unsurprising that many people choose survival, hoping that honesty and integrity will one day triumph. On the other hand, in *Persepolis* those who sacrifice their lives for their principles affirm the importance of psychological survival; they are an inspiration to others and reinforce the beliefs and values they uphold. Satrapi's experience also shows that some people survive and fight back, as she does through her memoir, by speaking publicly against oppression and injustice.

SAMPLE ANSWER

'The comic-book style of Satrapi's memoir detracts from the seriousness of the issues she explores.'
To what extent do you agree?

Marjane Satrapi's stark black-and-white illustrations in *Persepolis* are highly effective in conveying the horrors and tragedies of life in Iran, firstly under the Shah and then in the Islamic Republic. Yet the events she depicts are often so horrendous that Western readers, whose experiences are far removed from those in the text, might distance themselves from the characters' suffering. By drawing on readers' familiarity with the comic-book form, Satrapi encourages a wide audience to connect with her characters. At the same time, illustrations themselves are so dramatic that the gravity of the human rights abuses they depict cannot be ignored.

The illustration of the Cinema Rex fire is perhaps most deeply disturbing. Covering almost an entire page, the frame is dominated by ascending bodies, their ghost-like figures consumed by flames. Their facial expressions evoke the tormented figure in Munch's iconic composition *The Scream*. Like Munch's image, Satrapi's illustration conveys the subjects' pain and despair in a way that words cannot express, suggesting the utter obliteration of their humanity by the power of evil. Through Satrapi's mixing of comic-book and expressionistic art, she makes a serious political point about government brutality and injustice. This point is emphasised in images showing the sadistic cruelty of the Shah's police towards Ahmadi. He is savagely beaten, burned with an iron and, finally, cut to pieces. Satrapi's illustrations reveal the ruthlessness of the CIA-trained torturers, and of the brutal regimes they serve. The presentation of these atrocities in comic-book style invests the genre with a seriousness that moves beyond traditional conflicts between fictional heroes and villains, where goodness (embodied in the 'hero') eventually triumphs over evil. In the grim reality of Satrapi's world, heroes usually die. The death of Anoosh, Marji's 'hero', casts her adrift in the blackness of space, where her overwhelming sense of loss evokes a universe utterly devoid of hope.

When sharia law is enforced in the Islamic regime, Satrapi invites readers to relate strongly to the characters through illustrations highlighting people's loss of individual freedom. Strong visual images reinforce written words: compulsory breast-beating and self-flagellation rituals, where people act in unison, suggest the mindlessness of these actions in a way that verges on mockery of the regime that enforces them; yet, at other times, unity of action illustrates people's free will and shared values. Opposition to the Shah is expressed in illustrations of protesters acting in unison, revealing their commonality of purpose, while the horizontal band of almost-identical dead protesters on the next page unites them in their willing sacrifice. 'One massacre after another' follows, with images of similarly drawn victims, underlining the importance of protest despite the loss of life. Moreover, the eventual overthrow of the Shah ultimately validates the people's right to freedom of speech. In the Islamic Republic, where many people adopt fundamentalist views, freedom of speech or expression is more dangerous. Individual acts of resistance, such as Marji wearing a denim jacket and Michael Jackson badge, are very risky. Marji's terrifying ordeal with the Guardians of the Revolution – shown in successive images of two fierce fundamentalist women intimidating a defenceless child – and the threats of rape against Taji for not covering her hair reveal people's powerlessness to challenge oppression in the Islamic Republic.

The importance of significant symbols in the text is also emphasised through Satrapi's artwork. The white swans made by Anoosh during his imprisonment symbolise beauty and show his refusal to be crushed by his tragic fate. By including the swans in the frame with the newspaper announcement of his execution as a 'Russian spy', Satrapi celebrates Anoosh's gift for artistic expression and condemns government propaganda and injustice. Also powerfully symbolic are the golden keys given to sons of the poor. A large frame showing young boys dying with keys around their necks highlights the government's willingness to sacrifice them. The juxtaposition of their contorted bodies with those of teenagers from wealthy families dancing at a party (immediately below) implicitly condemns the slaughter of the socially disadvantaged in a war that 'could have [been] avoided'. Imagery of violent bloodshed recurs throughout the text, symbolising governmental injustice and cruelty. The agony shown in the face of Tinoosh's father, as he endures a beating so savage that he can no longer walk, evokes readers' horror and their pity for his suffering. Marji is similarly 'struck' by the 'gory imagery' of martyrs' blood being injected 'into the veins of society'. Satrapi's illustration undermines the government's patriotic propaganda: the figure representing society appears to absorb the martyrs' pain rather than being reinvigorated by their blood.

The comic-book genre is used effectively by Satrapi to accentuate rather than counteract the seriousness of the moral and social issues arising from the oppression of people under a totalitarian regime, whether it be a corrupt monarchy or a repressive theocracy. In doing so, she invests the genre with a powerful political dimension which is heightened by the expressionistic features of her artwork. The widespread critical acclaim for the memoir shows how successfully Satrapi makes use of the comic-book genre to communicate her story.

REFERENCES & READING

The text

Satrapi, M 2003, *Persepolis: The Story of a Childhood*, Pantheon Books (Random House), New York.

Film

Persepolis 2007, dir. Marjane Satrapi and Vincent Paronnaud, Sony Pictures Classics. Starring Chiara Mastroianni.

Websites

Copley, J 2011, 'The New Global Literature? Marjane Satrapi and the Depiction of Conflict in Comics', *The White Review,* October, http://www.thewhitereview.org/features/the-new-global-literature-marjane-satrapi-and-the-depiction-of-conflict-in-comics/

Eberstadt, F 2003, 'God Looked Like Marx', *The New York Times,* 11 May, http://www.nytimes.com/2003/05/11/books/god-looked-like-marx.html

Lawson, E 2017, 'Coming of Age: The "Persepolis" Mixtape', *ComicsAlliance*, 31 March, http://comicsalliance.com/persepolis-mixtape/?trackback=tsmclip

Macnab, G 2006, 'Marjane Satrapi: of Madness and Mullahs', *Independent,* 26 July, http://www.independent.co.uk/news/people/profiles/marjane-satrapi-of-madness-and-mullahs-409478.html

'The Graphic Novel', *Marjane Satrapi: Persepolis,* https://satrapi1.wordpress.com/satrapi-graphic-style/